WITHDRAWN

HOW TO LOVE YOUR CHILDREN

Birth Order For Parents

By Clifford E. Isaacson

Algona, Iowa 50511

Published by the
Upper Des Moines Counseling Center, Inc.
Algona, Iowa 50511

Copyright © 1992 by Clifford E. Isaacson

Printed in the United States of America

All rights reserved. No part of this work covered by the copyright herein may be reproduced or copied in any form or by any means, graphic, electronic, or mechanical, including photocopying, recording, or informational and retrieval systems - without written permission of the author.

Library of Congress
Cataloging-in-Publication Data

Isaacson, Clifford E., 1934-
   How to love your children: birth order for parents / by Clifford E. Isaacson.
      p.   cm.
   Includes Index.
   ISBN 0-945156-03-0 (pbk.): $7.95
   1. Parent and child. 2. Birth order--Psychological aspects. 3. Parenting. I. Title.
HQ755.85.I79 1992
306.87--dc20

92-17298
CIP

–TABLE OF CONTENTS–

	Page
Introduction	1
The Parenting Predicament	5
How Birth Order Develops	7

BIRTH ORDER PERSONALITIES AND HOW TO LOVE THEM

The Only Child Personality	11
How to Love the Only Child	21
The First Born Personality	29
How to Love the First Born	37
The Second Born Personality	45
How to Love the Second Born	51
The Third Born Personality	59
How to Love the Third Born	65
The Fourth Born Personality	73
How to Love the Fourth Born	81

BIRTH ORDER PARENTING

Parenting as an Only	87
Parenting as a First Born	95
Parenting as a Second Born	101
Parenting as a Third Born	107
Parenting as a Fourth Born	113
When Nothing Works	119
Appendix	121
About the Author	129
Index	131

This book is dedicated to the parents who want to love their children.

The illustrations are by artist
Steve Brosnan of Algona, Iowa

HOW TO LOVE YOUR CHILDREN

Birth Order For Parents

INTRODUCTION

This book is not about disciplining, but about making children feel loved. It is about communicating love in words, putting love into action, and feeling love in the way you enjoy your children. The contents of this book will help you circumvent obstacles to loving which exist in you and in your children.

Parents need to use less discipline to raise children who feel loved than to raise those who feel unloved. When children feel unloved, the parent-child relationship is an adversary relationship in which punishment plays a major role. Perhaps failure to make children feel loved has spawned the current interest in how to discipline children.

If your way of loving violates your children's concept of love, you are likely to make them reject your love. Unless you understand that the way you express love might not appear to be love to them, you may resent them for being ungrateful. Consequently, when your children seem ungrateful, parenting becomes an exercise in discipline rather than an enjoyable relationship with them.

You might assume you understand your children because you have been with them from birth. However, if you think about it, you could discover you do not understand them as well as you think. You may not comprehend why they think, act and behave as they do. Rather than understanding them, you might be trying to form them into facsimiles of yourself.

The extent to which you enjoy your children reveals how well you understand them. In other words, if you un-

How to Love Your Children

derstand your children well, you enjoy them more than if you understand them poorly.

If you do not understand your children, you could feel victimized by their behavior. Without insight into their actions, you might be at a loss into how you can persuade them to listen, obey, or behave decently. More importantly, you fail to make them feel loved.

When feeling victimized by your children, you become impatient, speak out of anger, or threaten rather than parent effectively. From your role as their victim, you cannot enjoy them, nurture them lovingly, nor control them reasonably.

You may not realize it, but the child who exasperates you is simply expressing his or her personality rather than purposefully aggravating you. Until you understand your child and yourself, it is difficult to get beyond anger.

Understanding can be achieved through knowing the effects of birth order on your children and on yourself. Through birth order analysis you can comprehend why your children behave as they do and why you react as you do. And, through birth order you can discover how to improve the relationships between you and your children.

Birth order is a set of personality characteristics developed during early childhood to cope with one's position in the family. Once established, these characteristics persist for a lifetime, determining how a person views self, relates to others and understands the world in which he or she lives. Birth order consists of only child, first, second, third and fourth born.

Although birth order is not a new subject, the information in this book is new. The information was developed by comparing life patterns to birth order positions rather than simply working from the numerical positions in the family structure. Following the initial discovery of five-position birth order twenty-two years ago, I filled in the details while using the birth order concept in over 19,000 counseling sessions.

This book aims at enabling you to understand yourself, your spouse and your children in new ways. With this understanding, you have the opportunity to learn how to interact with others, especially your children, in ways which communicate love, gain a hearing, and confront effectively. Using your imagination, you can apply many of the principles of this book to adults as well as to children.

Introduction

If you like to experiment with human relations, this book suggests many ways to do it.

In order to use birth order effectively, it is necessary to correctly assess which position your child occupies in birth order. Using interventions or affirmations based on the wrong birth order position usually does not work, or it creates a negative rather than a positive effect. Consequently, it is important to identify which psychological birth order personality your child has, because it could differ from his or her chronological birth order. Be sure to read the chapter, "How Birth Order Develops", before you assume you know your child's birth order.

Since you may wax enthusiastic about the strategies in this book, please understand it is possible to overdo the suggested interventions. Using them too frequently can induce your child to react negatively rather than positively.

Try the strategies one at a time. After one works for you, try something else. By going one step at a time, you not only avoid overwhelming your family, you develop the skills you need to use the strategies.

Finally, as you delve into the chapters, realize it is okay to enjoy your children as they are. If you wait until they are perfect, you may not get around to enjoying them. And, in spite of whatever you do, there are no strategies which make you or your children perfect. There are only strategies to make life better.

How to Love Your Children

THE PARENTING PREDICAMENT

Parents are in a bind. They have less time with their children than did their parents, and their children are more sophisticated than were their parents' children. Parents do not have the time to learn by trial and error but need guidance in order to best use the time they have. Birth order can help provide the necessary direction for them.

The competition for their children's attention requires parents to be more astute than ever in communicating with their children. They compete with the professional on television who entertains their children, the school which controls much of their time, and peers who pressure them with their opinions. No longer can parents rely on the parenting patterns they learned in childhood to be effective.

Parents need to be wiser because their children can escape from them more easily than ever before. They can retreat into a television program, a video game, a friend's home, school activities, or into their own room. The parent normally does not have time to follow the child or the knowledge of what to say or do when they do follow. The old fashioned punishment remedies do not work as they used to. Threats are not effective. Even love seems to be elusive.

Parenting is difficult enough for two parents, but the problems are multiplied for the single parent. For the lone parent with no one to share the load, knowing what to say or do becomes doubly important.

Some people capitulate and hope for the best, but many parents continue to seek ways to succeed with their children. They do not want their children making the same

How to Love Your Children

mistakes they made for fear they may not fare as well. They want to pass on the wisdom they gleaned from their experiences, but they may lack the knowledge to communicate effectively with their children.

Children are different from each other. In spite of all that has been written about raising children, there is no "one size fits all" when it comes to communicating with them. Parents need to tailor their communication to each child in order to be heard, to create loving feelings, and, when necessary, to confront effectively.

Parents usually have a limited number of communication strategies which work with some children but not with others. When they use inappropriate communication techniques, they cause their children to rebel, to become depressed, to experience anxiety, to refuse to listen, to lie or simply to escape mentally and/or physically.

Many self-help books are not helpful because most seem to be written by people who are psychologically only children themselves. Consequently, they recommend techniques which often fail with other children. Furthermore, parents who are other than only children have difficulty applying many of these self-help techniques.

This book is designed to help parents understand and appreciate each of their children. When parents understand their children, they see their children as more reasonable than when they expect them to think, feel and act as they themselves would in similar situations. Through understanding, parents can provide a home in which their children learn to establish loving relationships, to achieve satisfaction in their lives, and to become emotionally healthy adults.

HOW BIRTH ORDER DEVELOPS

By coping with the unpleasant realities inherent in his or her position in the family, a child develops birth order characteristics. The only child copes with playing alone, the first born with the intrusion of a strange baby who usurps mother's attention, the second born with the first born who robs him or her of attention, the third born with the second born who derides him or her, and the fourth born with the third born who rejects him or her for being immature.

Birth order arises from these situations rather than from parents treating their children differently. However, in dysfunctional families, birth order effects are intensified as children are forced to cope with family craziness. Harmonious families allow children to develop much milder birth order characteristics. However, mild or severe, all children seem to adopt one of the five basic birth order positions.

From family to family, the pattern is the same for each birth order position. For example, in every family the only child has the problem of how to play alone without feeling lonely, the first born always feels unloved when mother "deserts" him or her for the baby, and so on. It is this pattern of experience which lends birth order its consistency. Since birth order is developed early in life, often within the first two years, gender differences do not affect a child's psychological birth order position.

In order to accurately identify psychological birth order, it is important to remember psychological birth order does not always equate with chronological birth order. For example, if the oldest child is five or more years older than the second child, the oldest child remains an only child psychologically. Furthermore, the second child also remains an only unless he or she loses attention to a third child. When he or she loses attention to the third child, the second child becomes a first born.

The oldest child also remains an only child though he or she is less than five years old when the second child is born, if a grandmother or other adult helps care for him or her during the first few days the baby is home. During those few days, the oldest child is protected from the loss of attention to the new baby until he or she grows accustomed to his or her second born sibling. This nurturing during those critical days asssures he or she remains an only, psychologically.

A child who dies may become included in the birth order if the child continues to be discussed as an imaginary member of the family. Because this child is included in the family psychologically, the next child accepts the next birth order position following that of the missing child. Sometimes, even a miscarriage counts if the anticipated child is psychologically included in the family.

Twins tend to organize themselves into consecutive birth order positions. For example, if twins are the oldest, one is usually first born and the other second born. Sometimes, they seem to take turns being first and second born, depending on the situation.

In blended families, children retain their birth order characteristics, once they are developed, regardless of their position in the new family. Adopted children also keep their psychological birth order positions if they developed them before they were adopted.

In larger families, birth order repeats with the fifth being first born, the sixth second born and so on.

In my experience, I have found that about one in four persons is an only child psychologically, one in four and a half is a first born, one in four and a half is a second born, one in six is a third born and one in eight is a fourth born. These figures probably vary from community to community, with close-knit or wealthy families having more psychologically only children because of access to assistance with the new born, and poorer families having more children in first through fourth born categories because mother needs to deal with the first born alone when the second baby arrived.

The only child develops his or her characteristics from solving two problems: how to play alone without feeling lonely and how to cope with unwanted, intrusive attention from parents and others.

How Birth Order Develops

The oldest child turns into a first born while he or she waits for mother to finish caring for the baby. The first born thinks mother no longer loves him or her because she gives priority to this little stranger whose slightest whimper takes mother away from him or her. Starting with the notion mother no longer loves him or her, the first born learns to perceive the world to be without love.

The second born becomes second born when the first born takes attention away by outperforming him or her. This child comes to feel inadequate at not being able to compete successfully with the first born. In addition to feeling inadequate, the second born also comes to believe no one cares about how he or she feels because the first born does not care about his or her feelings.

The second born causes the next child to become psychologically third born by trying to pass the feelings of inadequacy to him or her through ridicule. Whatever the third born does, the second born derides, pokes fun at and belittles. However, rather than feeling inadequate, the third born comes to feel vulnerable.

The third born tries to pass on the feelings of vulnerability to the fourth born by telling this child "You're not old enough to play with us". Rather than feeling vulnerable, the fourth born comes to feel both immature and unwanted.

The fourth born ignores the fifth child in an effort to pass on the feeling of being unwanted, causing the birth order to start over with the fifth child. If there are only five children, the fifth becomes an only child psychologically, even if the age difference with the fourth born is small.

Once birth order starts with a first born, there is virtually nothing a parent can do to keep the positions from developing in the children. However, if a parent sees to it that, starting with the first child, no child loses attention to the next baby, the children all remain only children rather than following birth order.

When all the children in a family are psychologically only children, a pseudo birth order develops. Each child tries to be different from the next older child, thus creating what appears, on the surface, to be birth order characteristics. In reality, the differences are variations of the only child personality. This is especially apt to happen in families who have the means to always have help when a baby is born.

We might wonder why the fifth child and younger are not onlies since there are older siblings who could care for them while mother cares for the baby. The reason appears to be that the older siblings do not protect the fifth child from feeling unloved because they are more interested in the new baby than they are in the fifth child. The fifth child probably feels the loss of love more intensely than a chronologically first born because he or she loses not only mother's attention, but everyone's as they turn away from the child to the new baby.

Occasionally, a mother can determine the psychological birth order of her first or second daughter. If the mother is under severe stress when her daughter is about age two, she can force her daughter to adopt the next birth order position following hers. In other words, if mother is a second born she causes her daughter to become a third born, or if mother is a third born she causes her daughter to become a fourth born. This never seems to happen with daughters beyond the first two positions, probably because with more than two children mother does not have the time to concentrate on any one child sufficiently to produce the effect. This exception to birth order happens rarely, but often enough that a person should be aware of it.

Even more rarely, a son's birth order can be determined by his father who is under stress while the child is very young. For example, in one family the first born son became third born because of his second born father's stress induced behavior toward the son when the son was two or three years old.

When a person's birth order characteristics contradict his or her numerical position, it is better to go with the displayed characteristics, even if there is no apparent explanation for the variation. For example, in one family in which the oldest child was third born psychologically, there seemed to be no explanation until mother remembered that at an early age her daughter had been cared for by a baby-sitter who had two older children. Her daughter seemed to have become third born in response to the baby-sitter's children. The children who followed the third born were fourth born, first born and second born, in that order. If a child's birth order remains a puzzle, experiment with different strategies for communicating with the child. By observing the strategies which work, you uncover the child's true psychological birth order.

THE ONLY CHILD PERSONALITY

More people are only children than one would suppose. In addition to only children without siblings, there are only children with siblings. For example, oldest children are onlies if their second born siblings came along after they they were old enough, age five or older, to keep from feeling unloved when their mothers attended to the babies.

Also, an oldest child remains an only if someone helps mother care for him or her until he or she becomes accustomed to the baby. Having become used to his or her new sibling, the oldest child does not feel cheated when mother gives her attention to the baby. Even a few days of grandmother's care allows the oldest child to remain an only if he or she learns to regard the baby as a sibling who belongs rather than as an interloper who takes away mother's love.

Furthermore, if the youngest child in the family is five years or more younger than the next older child, this youngest child usually is an only child. Because of the age difference, his or her older siblings do not interact with him or her so as to produce birth order effects. The third child is an exception in that he or she can be third born psychologically regardless of age difference, if teased or put down by the second born. Also, the fourth born may be fourth born psychologically in spite of six or seven years age difference with the third born.

Even with a small age difference, the fifth child will also be an only child if he or she is the youngest because the birth order starts over after the fourth born. In larger families, the ninth or thirteenth children will also be onlies psychologically, if there are no younger children.

How to Love Your Children

Whether the child is a true only or has siblings, the only child develops birth order characteristics by having to cope with parental intrusion and by having to find a way to play alone without feeling lonely.

Intrusion

The only child tries to solve the problem of intrusion by developing a fast speed for doing fun things before someone can interfere and a slow speed for allowing others the opportunity to help. The only child uses the fast speed to avoid interference when taking toys out of the toy box, when eating a piece of forbidden candy, or when going to the toy section at the supermarket. The child uses the slow speed to give someone a chance to assist putting toys back in the toy box, getting dressed, doing chores, or completing homework.

However, this strategy does not eliminate the fear of intrusion. The child feels threatened by unwanted intrusion throughout life. Even as an adult, the only may hurry through enjoyable activities and dawdle through chores. The fear of intrusion is experienced internally as a feeling of being unable to do what he or she wants because of things which "have" to be done.

The only child uses the dual speeds at home rather than away because it was at home the only child learned to feel smothered. Away from home, the only felt relieved from parental attention. The only child felt especially liberated at school where pressure was taken off because there plenty of other children vied for the teacher's attention.

Having experienced smothering at home, many onlies feel weighed down at home and liberated when they leave. Since they feel more free away from home, onlies usually communicate better when they are elsewhere. For example, an only is more apt to talk more when visiting friends or eating out than at home. Consequently, communication with an only is often enhanced by dining out, visiting friends, going for a ride, or taking a walk.

The adult only tends to feel life is all work and no play because he or she subconsciously distorts time through mental intrusion. He or she makes work seem long by thinking about having fun while working and makes play seem brief by thinking about work while playing. Consequently, an only experiences long weeks and short week-

The Only Child Personality

ends. A common only child complaint is "All I ever do is work. I never get to do what I want to do."

Onlies experience correction, suggestions and advice as intrusive. They often try to forestall this kind of intrusion by doing things "right" so others have no reason to point out errors, suggest improvements or offer advice. Fortunately, this propensity to do things right could permit parents to have more confidence in their only children, if they understood it. However, since only children tend to react emotionally to correction, they cause parents to assume the worst about their behavior when out of their parents' sight.

Because of their inclination to do things right, onlies are often judged to be perfectionists. However, onlies are not perfectionists because they do not try to get every detail right. They just want to do things correctly to avoid intrusion but details do not matter.

Since they dislike intrusion, you might think only children would adjust their thinking to make intrusion less onerous. However, onlies adopt a way of thinking which makes intrusion all the more discomforting to them. Rather than allowing for intrusion, they organize their time and space so encroachment feels disruptive. Consequently, they constantly brace themselves against intrusion into their worlds. Sometimes, they get headaches, sore shoulders and stiff necks from the resulting tension.

Organizing causes only children to regard equality as justice. If they perceive everyone has been treated alike, they feel justice has been served. For example, in order to be fair, only child parents give equal gifts of the same value to their children. Sometimes, they will not buy a necessary item for one if they cannot do likewise for the rest of the children.

Onlies organize by scheduling their time either mentally or on paper, constantly keeping it current. At any given time, onlies know what they will be doing in the next several hours, days and weeks. Intrusion disrupts the schedule, which onlies feel they must remake from scratch rather than simply adjust to new circumstances. You know an only's inner schedule is disrupted when he or she complains an intrusion "Has ruined my whole day".

Because of this internal schedule, an only usually responds with a "No" to requests which require a change in his or her plans. For example, an only child wife refuses her husband's invitation to go out to eat because she had plans to stay at home. However, after thinking about it, she might decide she wants to go out after she has had an opportunity to construct a new schedule.

Likewise, an only in charge of the family budget, says "We can't afford it" when the spouse wants to buy something. The budget is already made out without provision for the new purchase. However, given time to reconstruct the budget, the only finds a way to include the expenditure. A wise person always gives an only child time to adjust to intrusive requests.

When intrusion occurs, the only suffers discomfort even if the intrusion is minor. For example, when the only child comes home from school, he or she normally has the rest of his or her day planned. Being asked to take out the garbage constitutes an intrusion. Even though taking out the garbage requires only thirty seconds, the only child objects strenuously because this unexpected chore disrupts the time line in his or her head.

Your only child even tends to react negatively toward pleasant surprises which disrupt his or her schedule. For example, a surprise birthday party is an intrusion to the only rather than a loving, thoughtful act. Likewise, last minute plans to go out, unexpected company, or unscheduled demands to clean his or her room can be intrusive. And of course, unkept promises cause distress by fouling up the schedule in the mind of the only.

Many a child placed in an adolescent group home is an only child who comes from a single parent family. In this family, divorce not only disrupts the child's world, it introduces chaos as the single parent tries to make a life for him or herself and the child. Unable to cope with the chaos, the only child becomes more and more emotional, throws tantrums, pounds the wall, screams, smashes things, and reacts with extreme feeling to the slightest intrusive demand. The child, unable to get life organized in his or her own mind, may become so violently frustrated he or she makes it necessary for the parent to allow him or her to be placed in a foster or group home.

Even adult only children get frustrated coping with chaotic situations. Some onlies become so exasperated they punch holes in the wall, break up furniture, and even injure themselves by hitting or kicking immovable objects. They can become depressed if they have to contend with others who are undependable, who are frequently

The Only Child Personality

tardy, and who change plans unexpectedly without informing them.

Onlies often avoid intrusion by not asking for help, especially at home. Rather than asking, they drop hints by saying "There sure is a lot to do" or by making noise to attract attention while they are working. If that fails, they express their anger at others for not helping, but they express their anger after the chores are done rather than asking for help beforehand. A common conversation between spouses has the only saying "Why didn't you help me?" with the other responding "You didn't ask".

An only may subconsciously attempt to escape intrusion by avoiding the use of the first person pronoun. Rather than referring to self in the first person, an only uses the pronoun "You". For example, an only might say "You really get frustrated when people do not keep their word" rather than saying "I really get frustrated when people do not keep their word". An only may also use expressions such as "A person", "One", and "We" rather than "I" or "Me" when referring to self. For example, an only might say "A person really gets frustrated when people forget birthdays" when he or she is actually speaking of his or her own frustration. Subconsciously, an only hopes to minimize interference from others by referring to self indirectly.

Playing Alone Without Feeling Lonely

The only child solves the problem of playing alone without feeling lonely by creating imaginary companions. These made-up friends are invisible playmates, pets, toys or even parents. A parent becomes an imaginary companion by following the child's instructions to the letter during play, by saying and doing exactly what the child requests. In other words, with the parent's cooperation the child is able to project an imaginary personality on the parent. The parent becomes what the child imagines.

While playing with imaginary companions, the only child creates the whole relationship by thinking, feeling and speaking for both him or herself and the unseen friends. Consequently, the only child is not playing alone when he or she is playing with no one around. Parents may not realize it, but sending an only child to his or her room is not punishment because the child has friends there. He or she is not alone.

In playing with imaginary friends, only children create habits which persist for a lifetime. They learn to think, feel and speak for others, often frustrating those who try to relate to them. Instead of listening, onlies assume they know what others think, feel and plan, and they respond to their own assumptions rather than to input from others.

By being able to create their own companions, only children enjoy playing alone without feeling lonely. In fact, onlies can enjoy times alone throughout life, as long as they are at home alone. Subconsciously, they create friends of the familiar objects at home, friends which they keep them company when no one else is there. In order to have time alone, many onlies stay up later than the rest of the family or get up before they do.

Even in adult life, an only's imaginary friends have emotional significance for him or her. For example, an only might sorrow over trading in the old car which has become a friend. One only put her old cars into retirement on the farm rather than trading them in. Each has a name, a personality, and a special place in her heart.

To make an object into a friend, an only puts his or her mark on it. For example, a house becomes a home after the only child picks out a special wall paper, makes an addition to the house, or gets a special piece of furniture which makes the house a friendly home. Otherwise, the house remains just a house.

In raising an only child, it is important to understand the only's attachment to things. Otherwise, by getting rid of some "useless" item you might cause unnecessary grief to the only child. You may not relate to this kind of attachment to things but you need to realize it is of vital importance to the only child.

In relating to imaginary companions, only children develop a sense of the dramatic. For example, when telling stories, they put emotional expression into them. When reacting to events, they display passion. When relating to people, they do it with feeling. They use voice inflections, gestures, exaggerated descriptions and animated facial expressions. They are bubbly when they are happy and they are tearful when they are unhappy.

This tendency to be dramatic makes onlies interesting but it sometimes distresses parents who cannot comprehend why their children react to events with such strong emotion. Both parents and children become frustrated if parents try to make only children tone down their emotional expression. Parents who know the dramatic expressions of feelings originate in their children's imaginary relationships may be able to tolerate, perhaps even enjoy, their dramatic children.

Onlies often treat people as imaginary, repeating their childhood experiences by projecting thoughts, feelings and attitudes on them. For example, onlies tend to interrupt others in order to express their own ideas. They are not intentionally rude but they feel, since they already "know" what others think, feel and want, they do not need to listen to what others are saying before they express themselves.

On the positive side, the ability to relate to imaginary friends can be an asset. For example, many radio disk jockeys are only children who work by interacting with an unseen audience they create in their minds. Not needing feedback from their listeners, they interact dramatically with imaginary people, and thus they entertain those who are listening.

The tendency to project creates symbiotic emotional relationships for onlies with the important persons in their lives. Their feelings are tied to the feelings of others. When others feel good, they feel good as well. When others feel bad, they feel bad also.

To get over feeling bad when others feel bad, they think they must solve problems for others or, failing that, try to persuade others to feel better. If they fail to fix problems and if they are unable to persuade others to feel better, they become exasperated. If they perceive others want to continue talking about problems, onlies may retort "I don't want to hear about it. There's nothing I can do." Often others protest, and rightfully so, by saying "I didn't ask you to do anything".

Because onlies want to fix things, they tend to be poor listeners when others express negative feelings. Rather than listening, they try to solve problems prematurely and without regard to what others really want from them. They may not comprehend that others just want to express their feelings rather than to get help with their problems.

Feelings

Only children value feelings in their decision making, relationships and planning. They think with their feelings. They reach decisions through feelings. They evaluate ideas according to how the ideas feel to them. They relate to people according to emotions inspired by them.

When making a decision, onlies try to anticipate how they are going to feel before deciding. For example, one man in a marital crisis, could not decide if he wanted to stay married or if he wanted to get divorced because he could not tell how he was going to feel in either case. He procrastinated over his decision because he could not figure it out.

Onlies think with their feelings by worrying. They worry to keep traumatic events from happening. They worry to make things come out right. For example, one adult only child felt bad because she had forgotten to worry about a fellow employee who was having surgery. She felt she had let her friend down because, by not worrying, she had not supported the successful outcome of the surgery.

Onlies often use emotion in the form of tantrums to control parents. Even in adulthood, onlies may indulge in outbursts of anger by throwing objects, slamming doors, and screaming at family members. Though most onlies do not throw tantrums as adults, it is more natural for them to use emotion than persuasion in dealing with other people.

Because onlies regard feelings as powerful, they try to avoid feelings of disappointment. In their attempts to escape disappointment, onlies choose to become pessimistic by thinking they are not going to be as disappointed by a letdown if they do not let their hopes get too high. Onlies who are trying to protect themselves from the pain of letdowns look on the dark side of things, expect the worst and reject suggestions that things will work out. They are not going to let themselves feel good until things actually work out.

Onlies do not see themselves as controlling their own feelings. Rather, they believe their feelings are controlled by circumstances, events, and other people. Consequently, they often adopt the attitude that "If the world would change, I would be okay". With this attitude, they demand other people change their ways so they, the onlies, can be comfortable.

Paradoxically, even though they believe their own feelings are governed by forces outside themselves, they think others can change their emotions any time they want. Consequently, onlies tell others how to feel and become frustrated when they do not immediately adjust their feelings accordingly. Sometimes, by demanding the "right" feelings from their spouses, onlies unconsciously encourage their spouses to feign the "right" feelings to placate them.

Onlies usually regard emotion as the primary motivation for doing things. This means anything onlies do not feel like doing, such as chores, is something which "has to be done". Onlies cannot conceive wanting to do something they do not feel like doing. Only children reflect this thinking by asking "Do I have to?"

Attitude toward emotions also determines how onlies approach a task. They determine how they feel about a task by viewing it as a whole, and they approach the task emotionally according to how it looks in its entirety. If the task appears huge, they feel overwhelmed by it. If it appears distasteful, they are repulsed by it. If the task appears enjoyable, they are eager to get at it.

Since they take a task in its entirety, they also feel they must have the time to do it all at one time. A three hour job needs a three hour slot of time and cannot be done in several segments. Consequently, they frequently procrastinate when they are unable to do an entire job at one time. They finally do the task when the pressure of deadlines compels them to get it done whatever way they can. Procrastination forces some onlies to function under pressure much of the time.

Summary

Only children develop their birth order personalities by creating imaginary companions with whom they play and by developing two speeds which they use to ward off intrusion. Out of these two coping strategies arise the only child characteristics.

Only children become organizers, fixers, and dramatizers. They enjoy time alone, are sensitive to interference, worry, and try to do things right to avoid so-called constructive criticism. They react rather than interact, feel pressured at home but free away from home, and absorb others' emotions into themselves.

How to Love Your Children

" I don't know about you, but I like what you've done."

HOW TO LOVE THE ONLY CHILD

Interventions

The only child can be difficult. Just when you want to get close, the child pushes you away. When you want to tell the child something, he or she has something to say and does not listen. When you want to give the child a pleasant surprise, the child becomes offended.

How do you love a child who retreats into his or her own world, reacts rather than interacts, and does not like to be surprised if the surprise interferes with his or her space or time? You must find the way into this child's world before you can make this child feel loved.

You can penetrate the only child's privacy barrier by professing ignorance of this child's thinking, feeling or desires before you communicate your thoughts, feelings or desires. For example, if you want to invite the child to go to the park you might say "I don't know about you, but I would like to go to the park today". The words, "I don't know about you", raise the only child's comfort level to enable communication to happen easily without the child feeling defensive.

By saying you do not know about the child's thoughts or feelings, you make your following comments non-intrusive by respecting the child's privacy. You increase the likelihood of your child listening. The child may not want to go to the park with you but he or she does not automatically reject your invitation as intrusive.

An only child tends to respond to emotional statements with logic and to rational statements with feeling. For example, if you tell an only child "I don't feel like going shopping today", the child is apt to give you logical reasons for going shopping by calling attention to sales, telling you why this is a good time to go, or reminding you plans have already been made. However, if you preface your words by saying "I don't know about you, but I am too tired to go shopping today", the child is apt to respond to your feelings by asking if you would go later after you have a rest.

When you make a rational statement an only is apt to respond with emotion. For example, if you say to an only "I think you should get at your homework", he or she may react emotionally by saying "I don't feel like it right now" rather than rationally by saying "I will do it later". However, if you were to say "I don't know what you think, but I think you should get at your homework", your reference to thinking is more apt to elicit a rational response such as "I'm going to do it at 8 o'clock".

These approaches to the only child create a feeling of being loved as well as getting the kind of response you want. However, it is best to limit the frequency with which you use them to keep them effective. Furthermore, there is no need to use these interventions often because they cause the child to respond more positively for hours and sometimes for days.

Sometimes, you can slip these interventions into a conversation innocuously. For example, you can comment "I don't know about you, but I really like this ice cream". This statement, made in passing, can increase the only's comfort level without the child's awareness and create a feeling of being loved.

These interventions work with only children of any age and with adults. You may enjoy using them to develop rapport with all the significant onlies in your life.

Another way to make onlies feel loved is through keeping promises, especially with regard to appointments. Since onlies keep a schedule in their minds, they are aware of how punctual you are. Keep your promises and you make onlies feel you care; break your promises and you make them feel you do not care. When you break a promise you force onlies to redo their entire schedules, much to their discomfort. If you cannot keep your promises, you can minimize the effect by keeping the only informed of changes.

An only feels good when you give him or her as much advance notice as you can. For example, instead of saying "Please put out the garbage" you can say "Please put out the garbage after school", so your child can plan for it. Even though the chore only takes a few seconds to perform, an only regards it as an intrusion if he or she could not plan for it in advance. Moreover, the child may choose to do the chore immediately to keep from having to think about it later.

Onlies tend to dislike surprise parties because surprise parties are intrusive. If an only child comes home from school to a surprise birthday party, the child's first reaction, at least internally, is that it interferes with his or her plans for the evening. Consequently, the child protests he or she had plans rather than bubble with the joy which you anticipated. The child is happier if he or she helps plan a party or at least realizes it is going to take place.

Because you see an only child to reacting emotionally to changes, you are tempted to put off informing the child about unpleasant events coming up. For example, you wait till the last minute to tell him or her about feared dental appointments, about visits by cousins he or she despises, or about having to go to the baby-sitter. The effect of this delayed communication can devastate the child since he or she cannot incorporate the change into his or schedule before it takes place. Notified at the last minute, the only child experiences the stress of change with no chance to prepare for it.

Rather than putting off telling, you can calm the child by saying "You can be angry if you want, but that does not change the situation". For example, a Sunday School teacher who had a second grade student given to striking the other children, required him to take a time out by sitting on a chair in the hallway. As she was escorting him to the door he screamed his protest at the top of his voice. After other strategies failed, she informed him he could scream if he wanted but he would still have to sit in the hall. He looked at her in surprise, quit screaming, and took his chair to sit outside the door. Later, when he forgot himself and hit another child, she put him out again. This time, he picked up his chair and went out willingly.

Since onlies tend to believe the world should adjust to their emotions, it is good for them to learn early on that responsible behavior rather than feelings influence circumstances, events and people. If you, as a parent, respond to rational behavior rather than to emotional outbursts, you encourage your child toward rational behavior. Of course, some people can always be manipulated by emotionalism, and onlies get their way with these people.

The words, "You deserve", can help an only feel loved. For example, if your only child son has been working hard at mowing the lawn, you can say "You deserve a break". If your only child daughter wants to try out for cheerleading, you can tell her "I think you deserve the chance to try out". These words can create a warm feeling of being loved in the only.

If you must confront the only child, you can also do so most effectively by referring to his or her thoughts first. For example, if you want the child to go to bed you might say "I know you want to stay up longer but it's bedtime". Or, if you do not want your son to take the car you can say "I know you would like to take the car, but we need it tonight". The child might not like the decision but adjusts to it better than if you simply said "No". Thus, even in confrontation you can make the only feel you care about him or her.

Perhaps the simplest way to convey love to an only is by giving him or her time and space. Allow the only to withdraw for periods of time to his or her room with the door closed. Unless you are an only yourself, you might fear your child is lonely, feels rejected, or is developing bad habits of withdrawal by being in his or her room alone. However, if you are an only you recognize an only feels loved as he or she enjoys time alone. An adult only gives him or herself this kind of solitude by staying up later than the rest of the family, by getting up earlier, or by encouraging the family to go out while he or she stays at home.

Allowing the only child to be alone enables him or her to indulge in the imaginary relationships which he or she developed when learning how to play alone. Forcing the child to always be in relationship to others deprives the child of this joyful experience.

Affirmations

You can help an only achieve control in his or her life by suggesting he or she can act in spite of feelings. For instance, when an only faces a task he or she does not feel like doing, you can simply say "You can do what you want even if you do not feel like it". This statement works best with onlies who are young enough to accept what you say without question. Older children may argue that wanting to do something and feeling like doing it are the same thing. In that case, instead of saying it, you can ask "Is it okay for you to do what you want even if you do not feel like it?" in order to elicit a decision. The decision gives them freedom to act rationally when necessary rather than emotionally.

It probably seems odd to suggest children act against their feelings, but doing so enhances self-discipline. By being able to set aside feelings they can do what is necessary, like homework. A child does not have to feel like doing it to do it.

If the child seems to equate "wanting" with "feeling", you can explain the difference is we want to work and we feel like playing. We want to work so we can support our lifestyle even when we do not feel like doing it. For example, you can explain to your child you want to do the dishes even if you do not feel like it because you want clean dishes for the next meal. At first, the child might be puzzled by the difference between "Wanting" and "Feeling" but, hopefully, comes to realize he or she does not have to be governed by feelings in doing things.

You can also suggest the only child can ignore feelings, even though popular opinion demands we be in touch with feelings (a concept probably promoted by adult only children). Ignoring feelings enables an only to practice self-discipline to his or her own benefit without having to make him or herself do things, i.e., overcome negative feelings. With practice, the only learns to feel good doing what used to be an emotional burden. It takes less energy to ignore feelings than to suppress feelings.

You can help your only child feel better when he or she is upset by stating "You can feel bad if you want, but you

How to Love Your Children

don't have to feel bad just because things are bad". Perhaps this statement sounds harsh to you, but telling the child he or she does not have to feel bad liberates the child from being an emotional victim of circumstances. Otherwise, the child may have to live with a rule which says you must feel bad when situations are bad.

Only children tend to worry. If you want to relieve your only child of the burden of worry, tell him or her "You can worry if you want but it won't change anything, so it's okay to take things as they come". While this statement may not produce instant relief from worry, you have introduced the possibility of accepting things as they occur rather than trying to control them through feelings. It is the caring thing for you to do.

Only children hate to be corrected. Consequently, they often try to do things so well no one can improve on it. While doing things right is pleasing to you as a parent, it might force your child to be overly cautious about what he or she tries. In other words, to escape intrusive suggestions the only child tries to avoid making errors. At the proper time, when your child is agonizing over trying something new, you want to inform him or her "It is okay to take the chance of making a mistake so you can try new things". By so saying you expand your child's potential for achievement. He or she will not be limited to doing those things he or she already knows how to do without making mistakes.

When he or she is feeling bad over being corrected, communicate to your only child it is okay to enjoy being corrected. If your child is skeptical about enjoying correction, explain that being corrected is an opportunity to do things better. Furthermore, by deciding it is okay to enjoy being corrected, he or she takes charge of his or her own feelings rather than permitting someone else to make him or her feel bad. Even when being corrected unfairly, the child can still enjoy being corrected if he or she gives self permission to do so.

Only children dislike requesting help for fear they might invite intrusion. Consequently, they often struggle over tasks for which they could get help, if they but asked. So your offer of help may not appear intrusive, phrase your offer by saying "I don't know if you would like help but I would like to help you with that". In so saying, you make your offer more welcome to your child.

To make asking more palatable, assure your child it is okay to do things his or her own way even after getting

In trying to exact respect at home, first borns can be obnoxious to family members. For example, first borns may mistreat younger siblings if they do not "respect" them by giving in to them, by agreeing with them, or by anticipating what they expect. They sometimes pout if their parents do not give in to their demands or agree with them.

First borns also get irrationally angry at inanimate objects which do not work because they do not get "respect" from the objects. And, of course, they can get angry at animals or pets who do not yield respect by being obedient to them.

On the other hand, a first born away from home treats others with the utmost respect as he or she tries to gain their admiration. He or she compromises with them, says what he or she thinks they want to hear, and tries to impress them. Consequently, a first born appears to be a different and much nicer person away from home.

In order to get approval, your first born child might be anxious to please his or her teacher. He or she tries to anticipate what the teacher wants and seeks to supply it. If unable to get approval, as from a second born teacher for instance, he or she can become depressed.

Sometimes, first borns are obnoxious toward authority if doing so impresses their peers. For example, if first borns belong to a gang where such behavior gains approval, they can be offensive to authority figures.

Lacking permission to love themselves, first borns lose touch with what they want. In order to protect themselves emotionally, first borns subconsciously block out their desires because knowing what they want without freedom to get what they want would hurt. Although frustrated, they subconsciously feel safer being ignorant of what they want. When asked about desires, first borns often reflect this ignorance by saying "I don't know". The statement "I don't know" can become an automatic response from a first born. It can be said so quickly it comes out "I dunno". Often, a first born starts telling something by saying "I don't know, but...".

Sometimes, first borns do know what they want but claim ignorance until they see what others think. They try to discover what others think by hinting at what they want. In other words, they put up trial balloons to get reactions.

First borns tune in to what other people think and feel rather than tuning into themselves for direction. Not knowing what they themselves want, they wait until they know what others want before deciding. For example, when eating in a restaurant, first borns do not know what they want to order until they hear what their companions want. If they should order first, they may regret their choices when they see what others get.

First borns welcome praise as conditional love and are more apt to believe it than expressions of love. However, because they accept praise for doing things well, they also anticipate condemnation for doing things poorly. After all, praise is conditional and can be lost at any time. Consequently, they often agonize over the thought someone might discover something with which to censure them. Unable to put personal failings into perspective, first borns live with a psychological Damocles Sword dangling over their heads.

Because first borns crave praise and fear condemnation, they may resort to exaggeration or lying to achieve praise and to avoid condemnation. However, even as they stretch the truth they increase their anxiety over the possibility of being found out.

Yearning for praise, admiration or approval, first borns often imagine that if they could just accomplish great things, they would get people to like them and to forgive them for their shortcomings. To get people to like and forgive them before they accomplish great things, first borns share their dreams of greatness with others with the hope of impressing them and distracting them from any judgment they might feel. Consequently, first borns often appear boastful.

Your first born child frequently daydreams about future achievements, especially when under pressure, rather than doing the necessary work to move toward objectives. As he or she daydreams, your first born hears the accolades, accepts the rewards, and basks in the warmth of admiration. For him or her, these fantasies make finishing tomorrow's math assignment mundane fare compared to the wonderful experiences which have already taken place in the privacy of his or her imagination. Thus, fantasies get in the way of true achievement.

Even when a first born does accomplish something, he or she immediately puts it into the past rather than celebrating its completion. He or she feels a sense of relief it is

The First Born Personality

done rather than a joy of attainment. He or she views tasks as a necessary evil to be gotten out of the way so one has time to visualize the scaling of new heights in the distant future.

Consequently, a "To Do" list fails to inspire first borns. The list acts as an onerous reminder of ordinary tasks rather than outlining steps on the path to greatness. On the other hand, a "Done List" of accomplishments encourages first borns to enjoy their achievements by helping them to pay attention to what they have done. If they can enjoy accomplishments, they are motivated to achieve more accomplishments which to enjoy.

First borns not only enjoy the future rather than the present, they also expect to have to do without rather than get what they want. Feeling unloved, they do not really expect others to give them anything unless they deserve it, and they are never sure they deserve it. Consequently, they do not even ask for what they want. When they do need to ask for something, they try to seduce people into giving by hinting at what they want. When hinting does not work, first borns usually give up rather than take a more direct approach. Furthermore, they might blame others for being unfair in not giving to them, even though they did not actually ask for what they wanted.

Sometimes, first borns become aware of what they want and their wanting becomes compulsive. They feel they must get what they want immediately because if they wait, they might not get it at all. They experience a kind of tunnel vision which focuses narrowly on the desired object but which keeps them from seeing the object in the context of other things they could have. Unable to prioritize their wants, they compulsively acquire something only to discover they do not want it after all. Meanwhile, they made an excessive sacrifice to get it. For example, a first born may buy an expensive car without considering what he or she has to give up in order to make payments.

The tendency of first borns to compromise away what they want often frustrates concerned parents. They see their first borns go along with peers' desires rather than asserting themselves. Parents are further frustrated as they see their first borns refuse to compromise at home. Unless parents realize this paradoxical behavior of demanding respect at home but catering to others away from home springs from seeking the substitutes for love, they can feel hurt or enraged by this behavior.

The demand for respect at home can be so disruptive a first born ends up in foster care because his or her behavior becomes intolerable for the family. The first born's behavior becomes especially unacceptable when he or she abuses younger siblings.

First Born Thinking

When you see your first born staring into space, you wish you knew what was going on in his or her mind. You wonder what he or she could possibly think about which could occupy so much time. You might wonder if fantasy could be good for the child.

When a first born sits staring into space, watches television without paying attention to it, or is lost in thought when others are talking, he or she is probably rehearsing. He or she could be having a conversation with a teacher who is pleased with a piece of work he or she is going to turn in, he or she could be getting praise for a brilliant idea he or she is going to contribute to a group, or he or she could be enjoying an accomplishment years in the future. On the negative side, the first born could be suffering a reprimand from a teacher for not getting homework right, could be getting ridicule from friends for having the wrong kind of haircut, or could be experiencing pain for appearing stupid before peers.

Since the first born lives in a world without love he or she creates a secret world of conditional love. In the privacy of the imagination the first born enjoys respect, admiration and approval. Within the mind he or she impresses people, repels insults, makes wise observations, and accomplishes amazing feats.

However, the secret rehearsals of the first born do not enhance his or her relationships with people. Rather, they create a handicap by setting a stage which does not correspond to real life. Since the rehearsals do not accurately represent how others behave, they do not prepare the first born for encounters.

Since negative as well as positive encounters can be rehearsed, a first born often rehearses embarrassing situations. If a first born thinks he or she has done something which could be embarrassing if discovered, he or she rehearses the scene, suffering more agony privately in the mind than he or she experiences in real life. Sometimes, as a result of the rehearsing, first borns go overboard explaining their behaviors as if they were actually being judged.

Loving

In addition to seeking respect, admiration and approval as substitutes for love, first borns try to use them as means of loving others as well. In other words, they extend respect, admiration and approval to others, and they hope others regard those things as love. Usually, they do not succeed in making others feel loved because they are using substitutes other birth orders do not regard as love.

If the first born is not in a position to extend respect, admiration and approval, he or she simply agrees with the other person. If the person says "Black is white", a first born tries to figure out a way to agree that black could be white. For the first born to disagree with anyone is to risk losing whatever love the other person might have for him or her. Love is too rare a commodity for the first born to risk.

Obviously, a person who always tries to agree with everyone is seen as wishy-washy. People soon come to realize the first born, like a chameleon, takes on the color of his or her surroundings. He or she has no color of his or her own. Consequently, the first born is subject to the peer pressure of companions rather than being the leader you might expect the first born to be.

Summary

A first born becomes a first born by losing attention to the baby and therefore, lives in a world without love. His or her strategies are built to cope with lovelessness. These strategies include finding conditional substitutes for love in respect, admiration and approval, being agreeable in order to conserve whatever love is available, and protecting him or herself against lovelessness by concealing his or her own desires. A first born believes others do not care about him or her, feels there is no mercy for him or her, and finds it hard to show genuine affection to others.

How to Love Your Children

suggestions. Thus, advice feels less intrusive when your child feels free to follow his or her own ideas rather than having to carry out someone else's ideas. As your child finds it easier to ask, he or she can call on other people, such as teachers, for assistance.

Quite often, only children feel restricted from doing what they want to do. They often reflect this feeling by complaining, "I never get to do what I want to do", which might sound ludicrous to you. However, onlies feel life is full of things which have to be done, with little time to do what they feel want to do. You can liberate onlies by assuring them "It's okay for you to do what you want". You might be surprised by your only protesting that he or she has too many things that "have to be done" to be able to do what he or she "wants" to do. Their tyrants live within them.

If you are reluctant to tell your child it is okay to do what he or she wants, realize that, as a parent, you set the boundaries for your child. It is within those boundaries your child may do what he or she wants. For example, you tell your three year old, whose boundaries are the borders of the front yard, "You may do what you want". The child can ride the tricycle, play in the sandbox or throw the ball within the limits of the yard. When the child is older, the boundaries will be wider.

Onlies often attach their feelings to others' emotions, much as they tied their feelings to those of their imaginary companions. Consequently, onlies are happy when others are happy, unhappy when they are unhappy. You can liberate them from the tyranny of others' feelings by giving permission to feel happy even though other people are unhappy. To strengthen the thought, you can explain it is easier to help others when feeling good than when feeling bad.

If your only child often acts pessimistic, he or she is probably trying to protect him or herself from disappointment. Being let down feels like a major emotional trauma, which the child hopes to escape by limiting hopes to prevent a drastic emotional fall if hopes are dashed. To help your child be optimistic, affirm that he or she can handle disappointment and therefore, it is okay to take the chance of being let down. With this affirmation, your child learns to survive disappointment as a natural part of life without trying to protect him or herself from it.

Onlies hate being interrupted and react negatively to anyone intruding on them when they are occupied. You can help onlies change their reactions by suggesting "It is okay to enjoy being interrupted. There is nothing about being interrupted which says you have to feel bad." While this idea might sound strange to onlies, it helps liberate them from having to feel bad over being interrupted.

As your only child gets older, he or she tends to organize not only space and time but also people, including yourself. For example, your child tells you what to do about a situation rather than just listen to you. If you do not want this response from your child, you can tell him or her "I know how to organize, I just want you to listen to me". By saying this, you are apt to get a better hearing from your child and establish a closer relationship with him or her.

Summary

In summary, an only child feels loved when you recognize his or her autonomy, deliver him or her from the necessity of feeling bad, and liberate him or her to explore, experiment and discover. The strategies of this chapter enable you to love your only child in ways which make him or her feel loved.

THE FIRST BORN PERSONALITY

The first born child is born an only child and he or she remains an only until the new baby diverts mother's attention from him or her. Feeling rejected by mother leaving him or her to care for the baby, the first born concludes mother loves this newborn stranger more than him or her. With that decision, the oldest child becomes a first born psychologically.

Does not each child in the family lose attention to the next baby? Why is not every child the same as first born? The answer is that each of the other birth orders is already established in relationship to the next older sibling when the new baby is born so the loss of attention to the baby is not relevant to them. For example, the second born is already struggling with the feeling of inadequacy, so loss of attention to the baby is not relevant to this child's personality development. If the new baby has any effect, it is to make him or her feel more inadequate than before rather than feeling unloved. Loss of attention as loss of love to the baby is only relevant to the only child who becomes a first born in reaction to mother setting him or her aside for the baby.

However, children other than the oldest can be first born. For example, in the case in which the oldest child in the family remains an only, the next child becomes a first born if he or she loses mother's attention to the next younger child. Sometimes, when a mother requires help with the first three children, the first two children remain onlies and birth order begins with the third child who loses attention to the fourth child.

In families with more than four children, the child following the fourth born is an only child until the sixth child is born. Losing attention to the sixth child, the fifth becomes a first born psychologically, the sixth becomes a second, and so on. Thus, the birth order starts over and repeats in large families.

The oldest child, who is an only, becomes psychologically first born within a few days after the new baby comes home. The change from only child to first born occurs when the child makes the decision that mother loves this tiny stranger more than she loves him or her. He or she has stepped into a world without love.

Having felt he or she has lost mother's love, the first born comes to feel he or she has lost everyone's love. Thus, the first born's world becomes a world without love. He or she expects love from no one, does not love self, and does not know how to express love to others.

However, the first born does look for love. He or she discovers early that doing something for mother, like taking her the washcloth when she is bathing the baby, earns him a pat on the head which feels like love. Actually, rather than experiencing love, the first born has discovered conditional love.

As the first born grows older, he or she develops a set of substitutes for love in the form of respect, admiration and approval. Since these are given for performance rather simply being, they are conditional forms of love. For the first born, they are the love for which he or she craves.

When respected, admired or approved, the first born feels loved. However, because the feeling is based on conditional love it is transitory and needs to be continually recharged with more respect, admiration and approval. Thus, conditional love is like a drug which gives a momentary high but soon requires another "fix" to maintain. The first born never gets a lasting, satisfying feeling of being loved from the substitutes for love.

The first born searches for each form of conditional love in a different kind of relationship. The first born seeks for conditional love as respect from family where he or she expects siblings to obey and parents to agree with him or her. He or she looks for admiration from peers whom he or she tries to impress and with whom he or she must agree. The first born hopes for approval from superiors with whom he or she tries to agree in order to please them.

"You did very well, but I love you because you're you."

HOW TO LOVE THE FIRST BORN

Interventions

How do you love the first born child who thinks no one loves him or her? When you tell this child you love him or her, you are not able to make the child believe it. Your expression of love conflicts with his or her perception of reality.

Since this child does not believe love is possible, you have to take him or her by surprise to make him or her feel loved. Otherwise, the child trades off love for admiration. For example, imagine you are going to give your ten year old first born son a birthday party. You tell him you set the party for Friday, you are going to invite six of his friends, you plan to bake him a chocolate layer cake, and you will present him with a twelve speed bicycle. Rather than keeping it quiet, he trades your act of love for admiration by telling all his friends at school about the upcoming party.

When Friday comes, the party is anti-climactic. He has already collected his emotional "goodies" by impressing his friends. In fact, the party might be worse than anti-climactic for your first born if you are unable to deliver on all you promised. Suppose only five friends showed up, and instead of baking chocolate layer cake you bought a sheet cake, and you could only get a ten speed bicycle. He would be angry at you for your "lack of respect" and embarrassed to tell his friends the party was not quite the way he said it was going to be. He might even lie, if he thought he could get away with it, and say it was even better than he had thought it would be.

Suppose, instead, you gave him a surprise birthday party so he has no chance to trade it for admiration. Because it was unexpected, he would be happy with what you did, including the five friends, the sheet cake and the ten speed bicycle. He is more apt to perceive love in the surprise party love because he could not convert it into admiration from his friends.

Praise is a key to reaching a first born with love because praise is a form of conditional love which he or she believes. By giving praise before expressing love, you put a first born in a position emotionally to accept love. For example, you commend a piece of work the first born has done and, while he or she is basking in the praise, you affirm your unconditional love by saying "But I love you because you're you". This intervention is so effective it sometimes makes an adult first born tearful when it is used. Praise opens the first born up to hearing the word of love without letting him be able to reject it.

Even when you reprimand a first born, you can express love by saying "I disagree with what you have done, but I love you because you are you". Your first born would be surprised at your expression of love because he or she does not expect mercy, to say nothing of love, when he or she has done something wrong.

Confrontation is sometimes required if a first born abuses younger siblings in the process of demanding respect from them. You can confront most effectively by stating the child is being unfair to the younger children. For example, when one mother caught her seventeen year old daughter choking her younger brother, she confronted her by saying "It's not fair for you to treat your brothers and sisters that way. This is their home also and they

How to Love the First Born

have a right to be comfortable in their own home". The daughter stopped her ill treatment of her younger siblings.

It is important to use the word "fair" because other words do not work. For example, if the word "right" is used as in "It's not right for you to treat your brother that way", it would cause a first born to argue rather than to change behavior. Because a first born thinks in terms of fairness, he or she responds when that word is used.

Sometimes, a first born will behave obnoxiously in order to "prove" he or she is not loved. For example, suppose you punish this child for blatantly choosing to disobey. Having been punished, the child is "justified" in feeling unloved, even though he or she provoked the punishment.

However, the love the child was seeking was actually respect, which the child demanded in the form of being allowed to have his or her own way. In the first born's mind, not getting his or her own way is in indication he or she is unloved. This child pouts, screams, cries, or rages, not because you were unjust in your actions but in order to express his or her feelings of being unloved.

In this situation, you cannot change his or her behavior through punishment. However, you can thwart the first born's game by expressing unconditional love rather than punishing. For example, you might say "You can disobey me if you want, but I love you anyway" or "You can pout if you want, but I still love you". By such statements you challenge the first born to accept unconditional love instead of living in a world without love. Your expression of unconditional love could induce your child to discontinue the obnoxious behavior since you have taken away the reason for doing it by extending respect ("You can disobey me if you want") and love ("I love you anyway"). Nevertheless, the child might continue the behavior for a while to save face.

You can also get through to your first born by telling him or her you would "appreciate" a certain behavior. For example, a father, after asking his ten year old first born son three times to put on his shoes, told him "I would appreciate it if you would put your shoes on". Hearing it put this way, the son immediately responded by putting on his shoes.

The word "appreciate" probably works because it offers conditional love which the first born understands. The word "appreciate" directs the child's attention to earning the parent's love by obeying. While it may not work every time, especially if used too frequently, it works often. Sometimes, it works like magic.

If you should use this intervention with first born adults, realize it can irritate them. First borns tend to feel psychologically helpless when told "I would appreciate it if you would...". They generally feel compelled by the statement to do what has been asked, but internally they become angry.

If you want an opinion rather than the usual "I don't know" from your first born child, you can use the phrase "You may not agree with this, but I think...". In suggesting the first born could disagree with you, you are giving him or her permission to have his or her own opinion. He or she might surprise you (and perhaps him or herself!) by knowing what he or she thinks and being able to share it with you.

Sometimes, your first born disagrees with you in order to demand respect, especially if he or she can impress friends by disagreeing with you. Giving the child permission to disagree with you ("You can disagree with me if you want") tends to disarm him or her, making it difficult for him or her to use disagreement as a means of wresting respect from you. This permissive statement also takes away the opportunity to feel bad over not getting respect.

If a first born agrees with everything you say, the same permission works. Giving the agreeable first born permission to disagree enables him or her to agree with you by disagreeing with you. Consequently, the first born can have his or her own view rather than having to agree with you.

You can provoke your first born into making decisions by mentioning what other children are doing. For example, if you want your first born to put on a coat, you can tell him or her that other children are wearing coats. Your first born is more likely to do what he or she knows other children are doing.

Affirmations

Several affirmations relating to first born thinking, feeling and behavior express love to a first born. Even though they might not produce an immediate response, they give the child positive thoughts about self, others and life.

How to Love the First Born

Since your first born lives in a world without love, you can affirm love by suggesting to him or her it is okay to care about self. For example, when you see your son feels compelled to go along with what a friend wants to do, you can affirm "It's okay for you to care about yourself".

Of course, when you speak about self-love, give permission rather than criticism, commands, or complaints. For example, it is better to say affirmatively "It is okay for you to care about yourself" rather than "I wish you would care about yourself instead of always going along with what someone else wants". Giving permission to love self helps overcome the first born's perception of love having to be earned. Criticisms, commands, and complaints simply reinforce a first born's inability to care about him or herself, and tend to anger him or her rather than induce self-love.

Your first born naturally tends to feel bad when someone does not care about him or her. Of course, other children also feel bad when others do not care, but it is a special issue with the first born. A first born cannot shrug it off like other children can. You can help your first born child feel better by giving him or her permission to feel okay even though someone else does not care. For example, when your child has been mistreated, you can suggest "You can feel bad if you want to, but you don't have to just because someone did not care about you. It's all right to feel okay". By so saying, you relieve your child of the "necessity" of feeling bad when someone treats him or her unfairly.

Your first born tends to feel guilty when others dislike him. He or she expects to make everyone have positive feelings toward him or her, or at least to not feel negative toward him or her, and he or she believes it is just awful when someone feels negatively toward him or her. To escape this feeling, the first born needs to know it is okay to feel okay when someone dislikes him or her. You can convey the thought by saying, at the time he or she is feeling bad about being disliked, "You can feel bad if you want, but it is okay to feel okay when someone does not like you".

Commonly, first borns have trouble being happy or even thinking about being happy. They are so tuned in to what others think, feel, and want, they lose touch with being happy themselves. While you take it for granted it is okay to be happy, you are probably presenting a novel idea to your first born when you tell him or her it is okay to be happy. Tell your child it is okay to be happy, and you might see quite a change in mood in the child. To have the greatest impact, make this statement at a moment when he or she should be happy but is not.

If you see your son or daughter showing off to get admiration, you can suggest caring is better than admiration. It would be best to do this in ordinary conversation when your child could feel you are giving vital information rather than making a judgment.

When you tell your child about caring, he or she might protest no one cares about him or her. Rather than trying to convince him or her people care, it is more effective to accept the child's assessment and tell him or her "They may not care about you, but I care about you". Believing you care is a step toward believing others can care.

A first born often compulsively desires something which will mean little or nothing to him or her later. When your first born child is bent on getting something which is not a priority for the child, suggest "You can have what you want, but think about it. You might discover you would rather have something else." By so doing, you help your first born evaluate what is important to him or her.

If your first born would like to do something but fears doing it because someone might not like it, you can assure him or her it is okay to take the chance of offending others. After all, by trying to never offend anyone, he or she puts severe limits on what he or she can do. By taking the risk of offending others, a first born discovers people are not as easily offended as he or she imagines.

In case you worry that by giving permission to offend persons you could provoke your child into becoming obnoxious toward people, realize you are giving permission rather than commanding your child. Permission enables a child to be assertive; commanding encourages him or her to be aggressive.

Being rejected is painful to the first born because it arouses feelings of being unloved. Within his or her subconscious is a rule which requires him or her to feel bad when rejected. You can liberate the first born from this oppressive rule by suggesting it is okay to enjoy being rejected. Enjoying being rejected might sound strange to your first born (and perhaps to you) but it is possible to enjoy being rejected. In fact, it is to a person's best interest to enjoy being rejected because of the enhanced ability to respond. Feeling good enables a person to access inner resources more effectively than when feeling bad. Also, feeling good allows the first born to move on to other people who accept him or her rather than trying fruitlessly to win acceptance from those who reject him or her.

Summary

To love the first born means you must get around the first born's feelings that he or she is not loved. You need to find ways to surprise the first born with love, and you must affirm unconditional love in ways which he or she cannot reject. As you grasp the first born's world view, you will find additional ways of getting around the first born's resistance to being loved.

By using the affirmations in this chapter with your first born, you enable him or her to have a healthy, loving attitude towards him or herself and to accept love from others. With growth in giving and receiving love comes a healthier self-esteem for the first born.

How to Love Your Children

THE SECOND BORN PERSONALITY

The first born makes the next child into a second born by outperforming him or her. Motivated by feeling unloved, the first born takes attention away from the second child by doing things better, quicker and more elegantly. The first born has the advantage of age and is not above cheating to look better than the second born. For example, in a footrace the first born takes a head start on the second born to make the outcome more lopsided than just a simple win. In other words, the first born makes the second born's performance appear as poor as possible in contrast to his or her own.

Furthermore, to insure that parents or others notice the difference, the first born calls attention to his or her own exploits before the second born can get attention. The first born even speaks for the second born to keep the second born from speaking for him or herself. For example, the first born answers for the second born, given the chance.

As the children get older, the competition might not be as noticeable. In fact, as time goes on, the second born probably dethrones the first born by outdoing him or her in many ways. However, it is during the first two or three years that the crucial interaction occurs between first and second which causes the second child to be a second born psychologically.

In the face of the first born's attention seeking, the second born learns to think of him or herself as inadequate. It appears to him or her not only the first born, but anyone, can do things better than he or she can. Even when the second born obviously does things better, he or she feels someone could come along to put him or her to shame through superior performance. This feeling of inadequacy, which persists for a lifetime, underlies much of what makes a second born a second born.

The second born tries to resolve the problem of inadequacy by deciding that if he or she could just do something perfectly, he or she would be okay. However, rather than trying for perfection in every area, he or she chooses certain areas in which to strive for perfection. In those chosen areas, he or she strives to get every detail right.

Some second borns opt for perfection in the area of personal appearance. In their early teens, these second borns primp for hours in front of the mirror, practicing facial expressions, eye movements, and body language to get them just right. Usually girls, these second borns learn to talk with their bodies, faces, eyes and hands. They learn how to make their hair fall just so around their faces, to get makeup on exactly right and to coordinate clothes to be attractive in a slightly unusual manner. They have learned to make the best use of their attributes.

As adults, these girls are apt to be hired as receptionists because of their attractive personal appearance and demeanor. The first person you encounter in a doctor's office, lawyer's office, or in a business front office is often a second born who has done her body language homework.

Some second borns choose art, school work, cooking, sewing, woodwork, housekeeping or mechanics as their area for perfection. However, they do not try to do everything perfectly because that's clearly impossible. Because their perfectionism is limited it is rarely recognized.

Because of their perfectionism, second borns are interested in all the details in those areas in which they want to excel. They are dissatisfied with guesses, generalizations, or conclusions. They want to know the hard facts, the particulars and the details.

In outperforming the second born, the first born acts without love toward him or her, causing the second born to believe, and rightfully so, that the first born does not care about how he or she feels. The second born comes to believe no one cares about how he or she feels. Needless to say, this perception creates discomfort.

In order to exist in a world in which no one cares how he or she feels, the second born chooses to eschew feelings

The Second Born Personality

in favor of logic by reasoning "If I ignore feelings, I'll be okay". Consequently, the second born seeks to deal with all areas of life logically rather than emotionally.

Of course, no one is able to do away with feelings. At times, suppressed feelings break through like an emotional volcano, powerful and uncontrollable. When the eruption is over, the second born puts the lid to feelings and returns to being logical.

By setting aside feelings, second borns handicap themselves in communicating emotionally. For example, they have difficulty comforting, giving sympathy, or sharing joy. Second borns tend to offer help in the place of comfort, logical observations instead of sympathy, and compliments in lieu of joy.

They communicate thoughts and call them feelings by saying "I feel" when they mean "I think". For example, they might say "I feel we should take a trip" when they mean "I think we should take a trip".

Up to age twelve, second born children are often affectionate, open with feelings and responsive. After age twelve, they often become logical, critical and argumentative. Frequently, they begin to argue for fun. Naturally, their joy in arguing does not usually create a corresponding joy in their parents who look for compliance from them.

On the positive side, suppressing feelings makes a second born child the most self-disciplined of the children. By sheer willpower, he or she is able to stay on a diet, get homework done, or save money. He or she is able to stay on task until done rather than accept an invitation from friends to go play.

Second borns tend to avoid goals because goals are rooted in emotion. Instead, they pursue projects which can be accomplished by following a set procedure rather than pursuing goals which require the development of strategies to accomplish. By going from project to project, second borns can be very successful without having goals. They succeed if their projects add up to success. However, if their projects are mediocre, their success is mediocre. The starving artist is an example of a second born who pursues projects which do not achieve financial success.

A parent who assumes his or her children must have goals can get frustrated by the second born's tendency to focus on details rather than to pursue goals. The parent who insists on the child having goals can create conflict between his or her demands and the second born's desire to concentrate on here-and-now activities, and can generate feelings of low self-esteem in the second born who is unable to develop goals.

It is better for the parent to direct the child toward projects which will serve him or her well than to insist on goals. For example, rather than trying to direct a second born toward a career in computer programming, a parent can encourage the child toward learning computer programming. This learning leads toward a career naturally without having to impose goals.

As a consequence of their antipathy toward goals, second borns tend to not think about where actions can lead. For example, a second born child may not realize that turning down a friend who asks for help could cause the friend to refuse when he or she needs help.

An extreme example of second born inability to consider consequences is a man who, because he thought his wife was not disciplining their children properly, reported her to the Department of Human Services. The ensuing investigation probably was effective in curbing any possible tendency on his wife's part to abuse the children but it certainly wreaked havoc with their relationship. He had not anticipated how she would feel at what he had done nor that she could possibly leave the relationship because of what he had done.

In avoiding emotion, second borns often like to communicate by writing notes. Through using notes they can say what they want without risking emotional confrontation. They are likely to leave written notes even though they could have communicated in person.

Second borns tend to dislike deadlines because deadlines limit the time they have to spend on details which would allow the pursuit of perfection. Faced with time limits, second borns either finish tasks well in advance of the due time or they fail to deadlines. They complete tasks in advance to make time to pursue perfection or they procrastinate because they have despaired of achieving perfection.

Second Born Thinking

When second borns think, they evaluate everything in terms of whether it is good or bad, right or wrong, and whether or not it will work. This propensity toward evaluation apparently arises from the feeling of inadequacy which they try to overcome by evaluating self and others. Of course, the more they evaluate, the more they continue feeling inadequate.

Second borns communicate in judgments based on their evaluations. Even their humor is a dry sort of humor which sounds like criticism. For example, a second born might ask "Where'd you get that shirt, at a rummage sale?" with the expectation you would find the question to be funny.

Their response to another's achievements is usually not praise but an evaluation which includes suggestions on how to further improve performance. They tend to respond to new ideas by looking for pitfalls.

To others, second borns seem to be critical. However, second borns like to think they offer constructive criticism, or correction, rather than criticism. In fact, they usually feel hurt if someone calls them critical and they are usually very sensitive to being called nasty.

The second born problem solving technique is closely linked to their form of thinking. When things go wrong, they first try to establish who caused things to go awry and then, after expressing criticism, they proceed to try to solve the problem. The criticism is a defense against feeling inadequate. Consequently, second borns also criticize when they are under stress, rather than expressing their feelings of frustration.

Loving

Second borns express love by evaluating. When they care about someone, they offer constructive criticism aimed at helping that person toward perfection. The second born is, of course, assuming others are as interested in achieving perfection as he or she is. Unfortunately, since other birth orders do not take correction as an expression of love, they frustrate the second born.

Summary

Your second born child has learned to feel inadequate through the unfair competitiveness of the first born. He or she tries to solve the problem by striving for perfection in certain favorite areas. Also, the second born believes people do not care about how he or she feels and tries to solve that problem by being rational rather than emotional.

"True it's not perfect, but I love you anyway."

HOW TO LOVE THE SECOND BORN

Interventions

You might not be aware of when your second born craves love if you do not realize this child seeks affection indirectly rather than directly. The child's behavior does not speak directly to his or her desire for love. Consequently, unless you know what to look for you cannot "read" your child.

A second born believes his or her inadequacy makes him or her unlovable. When expressing feelings of inadequacy, a second born wants to know if you love him or her even if he or she is imperfect. By answering this unspoken question affirmatively, you convey love to your second born.

A second born commonly signals a desire for love by criticizing him or herself. For example, a second born who normally got good grades, told her mother her next report card would not be as good as previously. Mother thought daughter was worried about her report card rather than perceiving this statement as an indication her daughter wanted assurance of love from her.

Obviously, the child's statement appears to be a sharing of information rather than a bid for love, which is how her mother heard it. When the report card came, the grades were all "A"s and "B"s. Mother assured her the report card was all right and was puzzled when her daughter became upset. Actually, the daughter was not wanting to know that the report card was okay but that she was okay. She yearned to hear her mother say "I love you even though your report card is not as good as usual". Had she responded in this manner, the daughter would have felt loved.

If you recognize them, opportunities to express love to your second born child abound. When your child says "My nose is the wrong shape", "I just can't make this look right", or "I am no good at math", he or she has given you the opportunity to assure him or her of your love in spite of the negative quality he or she relates. When you hear your child put him or herself down, remember to say "I love you anyway".

Even if it should be your child is actually sharing information rather than asking for love, he or she will not be offended by your saying "I love you anyway". Your child will probably smile and go on with what he or she wants to tell you. When seeking love he or she reacts or makes a comment which indicates love is the issue. For example, your child might respond to your message of love by saying "Does that mean I don't have to take eighth grade over?" or "Does that mean I am not grounded?" and usually smiles.

Because of their perfectionism, second borns tend to see correction (but not criticism) as an indication of caring. They tend to view correction, or so-called "constructive criticism", as an aid to perfection. However, to be received positively, this correction has to be given kindly, without irritation, impatience, or put-down. If correction contains anger, it is no longer correction but criticism and irritates them.

Criticism is correction which is spoken with negative feeling. The second born is put off by the feeling rather than encouraged by the correction. Correction is given with positive feelings, and produces a feeling of being loved in the second born.

Consequently, one way to love a second born is to offer suggestions for improvement when he or she is doing well. Praise alone does not convey love to a second born, but praise followed by correction does make him or her feel loved. Rather than be offended, he or she perceives your suggestions as help toward perfection. If you are not a second born yourself, it might seem cruel to you to always "find fault" as it were. But, your second born believes you really care when he or she hears your suggestions.

For example, one school teacher was very popular with a second born student because, no matter how well he did, she always had a suggestion for improvement. Even though his homework assignment had an "A+" grade she still made red marks to show where he could improve. Consequently, he loved her because he perceived her as helping him toward perfection. His self-esteem benefitted from her corrections.

On the other hand, praise by itself can work negatively with a second born. If you give praise without pointing out flaws, you make the second born feel you are not being honest and you do not really care about him or her because you do not suggest improvements. For example, a second born who gets an "A" on a test might, if praised for it, do poorly on the next test. Making suggestions for improvement after a second born has done well motivates him or her to do even better next time.

To encourage a second born toward greater achievement, you must get around his or her perfectionism. Your incentive must not sound like it requires perfect performance from the child, or it will discourage the child. In other words, do not say "Just do the best you can" because the child will interpret the statement to mean "Do a perfect job". Rather, drop the "best" and say "Do what you can". The child then understands you are not asking for perfection but for performance according to his or her ability. The child may surprise you with his or her renewed enthusiasm.

Because of the tendency toward perfectionism, a second born usually wants to know the details about anything he or she is interested in. If told "You don't have to know everything", the second born feels unloved. Simply giving a second born details about things important to him or her imparts a message of caring.

Even an adult second born likes details. One man improved his marriage to a second born by keeping track of details during the day to share with her in the evening. He recorded things in a little notebook for reference before going into the house so he would remember what he wanted to tell her. Their marriage got better.

A second born expresses love in the same manner he or she likes to receive it. For example, when a second born sees you accomplish something he or she is apt to find fault with it and suggest improvements which could be made. Unless you realize your second born is actually communicating affection, you may resent the second born always "finding fault".

Of course, since other birth orders usually resent rather than appreciate constructive criticism, second borns can become discouraged in trying to establish loving relationships. They are confounded when others do not appreciate their observations.

If you become uncomfortable with second born criticism, you can curtail it by asking if he or she has any other criticisms. By asking for criticism you actually make it harder for him or her to criticize. However, this intervention frustrates a second born and should be used sparingly. It is better to view the criticism in a positive light than to curtail it.

A second born might enjoy arguing. His or her arguing probably frustrates you because you cannot win. If an argument ends in your being angry at your second born, you have lost an opportunity to make this child feel loved.

If you lose an argument, or especially when you lose, you have an opportunity to express your love to your second born. By saying "You and I aren't going to agree about this, but I love you anyway", you surprise him or her into feeling loved. Your second born will probably be at a loss for words or may simply mumble he or she loves you, too. However, underneath, he or she feels loved.

You can use this statement with second borns of any age. You can even use it with acquaintances by saying "You and I don't agree about this, but I like you anyway". You might be surprised at how this statement can enhance your relationships with second borns.

When your second born child abuses a younger sibling, you can confront him or her with "Think about how he (or she) feels". This statement almost compels a second born to consider another's feelings by linking thinking and

How to Love the Second Born

feeling in one statement, forcing him or her to think about feelings rather than ignore them. A second born cannot refuse to think about something when told to do it.

Another way to confront a second born who is arguing with you about doing something is to say "Do whatever you think is right". For example, a mother used this statement with her second born eleven year old who argued against going to bed. When she told him to do whatever he thought was right, he immediately went to bed.

Of course, in using this intervention you put yourself in a position of having to accept whatever the second born chooses to do. You need to be sure the risk is acceptable to you. In other words, you need to be reasonably sure he or she will do what you think is right also. This intervention should, like all interventions, be used sparingly because your child can develop an immunity to it with frequent use.

When trying to motivate your second born, you can save yourself frustration by using negative incentives. Unlike the other birth orders, he or she is more likely to be motivated by negative rather than positive appeals. In other words, a second born is more likely to be moved by what he or she is likely to lose rather than apt to gain, by necessity rather than possibilities, and by what could go wrong than by what could go right. For example, you are more likely to motivate your second born toward college if you suggest a college education is necessary to keep from losing out on employment opportunities rather than elaborating on the advantages of attending college.

Affirmations

You can use a number of affirmations with a second born to express caring. For example, when you see a second born struggling to stay rational you can say "It is okay for you to have feelings". This affirmation is appropriate for situations such as parties, family gatherings or funerals in which your second born should experience emotions. This affirmation helps release a second born from the necessity of having to be rational when emotions are a natural response.

Although second borns try to avoid emotions, they cannot escape feeling bad from time to time. You can help them be in touch with feelings by suggesting "It is okay for you to care about how you feel". In so doing, you not only put a positive spin on feelings but you give your second born permission to pay attention to his or her own emotions without feeling threatened by them. In fact, he or she might become able to comfort him or herself.

Often, second borns agonize over others not caring about how they feel. If you try to comfort them by trying to persuade them others do care, you could provoke resentment with your interpretation which flies in the face of their perceptions of reality. You comfort more effectively by assuring them it is all right to feel okay when people do not care about how they feel rather than by trying to comfort them through changing their perceptions.

Sometimes your second born becomes distressed because something is not perfect in his or her performance or in his or her world. You can help the child feel better by suggesting it is all right to feel good even when things are not perfect. By so doing, you help deliver your child from negative feelings over a flaw when the child expected perfection.

When second borns reject feelings, they subconsciously decide against putting themselves first because putting one's self first is an emotional act. Consequently, second borns tend to be self sacrificing, especially in relation to family members, because of their natural loyalty to family. To bring a balance between caring for family and caring for themselves, you can communicate to second borns it is okay to put themselves first, even before family. This allows them to choose whether putting family first or self first is appropriate in any given situation. For example, the child may want to put family first when a friend's invitation to play ball would interfere with a family trip and put self first when he or she would miss supper to be able to attend a special school event.

Furthermore, to bring a balance between logic and emotions to a second born, give him or her permission to put feelings before logic. You can make this affirmation when he or she is going to a party, on vacation or doing something for fun. To enjoy these situations he or she needs to allow feelings to predominate. When opportunity presents itself, tell your second born it is okay to put feelings ahead of logic.

Second borns typically try to avoid making others angry at them. Of course, most people do not relish having someone be angry at them but, for second borns, it is something to be avoided at almost any cost. Perhaps the

How to Love the Second Born

discomfort over anger as an emotion causes them to eschew irritating others. Whatever the reason, second borns may be unable to assert themselves for fear someone might become angry at them. In order to enable a second born to be assertive, you need to tell him or her it is okay to take the chance of making someone else angry.

Sometimes, rather than being unassertive, a second born offends people compulsively. Paradoxically, suggesting it is okay to risk angering others also delivers him or her from deliberate offensiveness. Once it is okay to do it, then it is also okay to not do it. Permission to anger people enables him or her to take conscious control of the behavior.

Finally, second borns are quite sensitive to criticism. To reduce this sensitivity, tell them it is okay to enjoy being criticized. Your second born probably regards this idea as a crazy notion but needs to realize that feeling bad over criticism gives others control over his or her emotions. Others can make him or her feel bad just by finding fault. By allowing him or herself to enjoy being criticized, the second born takes charge of his or her own feelings. Of course, because there is no perfection it is not always possible to enjoy being criticized.

Summary

Second borns tend to believe they must achieve perfection to be loved. By suggesting you love them when performance is less than perfect, you communicate love. Furthermore, by expressing love following a disagreement you create a feeling of being loved.

Since second borns try to eliminate emotions, you improve their quality of life by suggesting emotions are all right.

How to Love Your Children

THE THIRD BORN PERSONALITY

A child becomes third born when he or she experiences the second born trying to pass on the feelings of inadequacy by teasing, putting down and ridiculing him or her. The third born hurts as the second born unmercifully derides his or her feelings, efforts or ideas. However, rather than feeling inadequate, the third born comes to feel vulnerable. The third born comes to believe others can get to him or her any time they choose because the second born does.

As a parent, there is little you can do to keep the second born from harassing the third born. Typically, if you pressure the second born to stop, you force him or her to become more subtle rather than to cease harassing. You know the second born is still at it when you hear the third born get angry. Failing to get the second born to treat the third born more kindly, you probably recommend to the third born he or she just ignore the second born.

The third born tries ignoring the second born and discovers it works. By staying unruffled, the third born prevents the second born from getting to him or her. Upon this success the third born builds a defense strategy of not letting things bother him or her.

Actually, what the third born ignores is injustice. In ignoring injustice, the third born loses track of how to be fair to him or herself or to others. In addition, the third born develops a helpless feeling of sensitivity to being treated unfairly despite his or her resolve to not let it bother him or her. Of course, not letting things get to him or her does not constitute an adequate defense. Nevertheless, it is the best the third born has. He or she pursues it

How to Love Your Children

by trying to become invulnerable, reasoning that if he or she could just be strong enough, no one could get to him. Even if unable to be strong, he or she considers it important to make others think he or she is strong in order to fend off possible attacks. Quite often, a third born who appears strong feels very weak inside.

In order to be strong, a third born believes he or she must conquer fear because he or she cannot feel strong when scared. In combatting fear, the third born fights a battle in which he or she either wins or loses. If the third born wins by overcoming fear, he or she becomes fearless. If the third born loses to fear, he or she becomes fearful. Consequently, a third born tends to be either fearless or fearful.

Third borns can be fearless at one time and fearful at another, depending on the situation in which they are at the moment. Some third borns, by being fearless at one time and fearful at another, present themselves as a paradox to other people. How can a man who drives a semi in Chicago traffic be afraid of snakes?

A fearless third born must constantly prove his or her fearlessness. If a dare is extended, the fearless third born cannot reveal weakness by backing off. He or she must meet the challenge or else he or she has allowed fear to take power, and that is intolerable. Of course, for this reason many a third born gets into difficulty. For example, a third born boy was dared by his companions to steal an item from a store. To prove he was not afraid, he stole the item. He was caught, and he continued to "prove" he was strong by acting as if the resulting penalty did not bother him. Actually, he probably did not let it bother him.

Because of their fearlessness, third borns have the severest conflicts with their parents, particularly when they resist parental intimidation. These children must "prove" they are not frightened by the parents' threats. For instance, if a parent says "Be home by 9 o'clock, or you are grounded", third borns feel the need to demonstrate fearlessness by staying out past the set time even if they could have come home on time.

Since intimidation usually worked with the first two children, parents naturally assume it should work with the third born. If parents increase the intimidation by upping the ante for the third born, it becomes psychologically even more imperative for the child to "prove" his or her own fearlessness. In this contest everyone loses. Parents fail to control their child, and the child indulges in self-destructive behavior. For the sake of the child, it is essential parents understand the psychology of the third born and move away from trying to control by intimidation.

An adult third born might "fail" in a substance abuse treatment program which uses intimidation as part of the treatment. For example, one third born got himself ejected from alcoholism treatment twice even though he faced a possible prison sentence if he did not finish treatment. During treatment, when the therapists were trying to "get through" to him, he "proved" he was fearless by simply smiling at them. However, rather than seeing him as fearless, they saw him as uncooperative and expelled him from treatment.

Sometimes, third borns discover they can overcome fear by getting angry. Some third borns are angry much of the time as they replace fear with anger.

In his or her anger, a fearless third born attacks as a strategy for solving problems. Therefore, when confronted with a problem, a third born tends to penetrate directly to the heart of it in order to solve it. For example, a third born mother took an unexpected ride on the school bus to deal with older children who were abusing her children rather than waiting for school officials to solve the problem. Her way worked. It must have been a third born who said "The best defense is a good offense".

A fearless third born may suffer from boredom which results from turning off the fear. Fear is a natural stimulant which keeps life interesting. Fear is the active ingredient in excitement. Without fear, a fearless third born finds few things to be exciting. Even usually scary activities, such as fright movies, tend to be humorous rather than fear-inducing for the fearless third born. This fearless child is the most likely to complain that school, church, travel, work, family activity, and so on, is boring.

Quite often, third borns solve the problem of boredom by keeping busy. However, they cannot stop to rest for fear boredom will catch up to them. This may be a cause of Chronic Fatigue Syndrome in third borns.

The fearful third born is driven by fears. This child finds it difficult to take risks, to do things which might evoke ridicule, or to assert him or herself. This child seeks security by staying close to home, by clinging to parents,

How to Love Your Children

or by choosing familiar surroundings rather than venturing into the unknown.

As a child, the fearful third born is usually no discipline problem to parents. Parents have no need to intimidate the fearful third born into obedience because this child does nothing which invites reprimand. Rather, parents do well to push this child into activities which would be beneficial to him or her. For example, after they moved to a new community, one parent had to push his son to get a job, finish high school, and get a driver's license. This third born had retreated from the new, unfamiliar community to his room to watch television rather than to confront life.

The fearful third born might be anxious, have panic attacks and be apprehensive. He or she may worry, overprotect him or herself, develop phobias, or withdraw from encounters with people.

Third Born Thinking

Although third borns do not possess strategies for defending themselves, they do develop a kind of defense system from ideas and humor which they use to create space between themselves and others. While ideas and humor do not appear to others to be defense mechanisms, they do function as such for third borns.

Third borns feel less vulnerable if they can keep others at a comfortable distance by using ideas as a buffer. To accomplish this they generate ideas to distract others who are getting too close for comfort. While others are paying attention to their ideas, they feel safe. Of course, if others should reject their ideas they feel even more threatened. When ideas are rejected, they tend to get angry and can retain this anger for years.

Because of this felt need to produce ideas for self-defense, third borns are the most creative thinkers among the birth orders. They accomplish their creativity by making comparisons. Third borns compare parenting to managing a business, buying a car to making an investment, or planning a trip to preparing a meal. They compare a spouse's behavior to that of the spouse's parents, their children's behavior to that of their own siblings, or a friend's behavior to that of childhood companions. They compare life to a drive down a country road, love to a flower garden, or pain to a telegram bearing bad news.

Third borns understand new concepts and explain old ones by drawing on parallels from experience.

Comparing enables some third borns to become inventors by comparing functions and others to become poets by comparing ideas. As poets, they employ metaphors, a type of comparison, for their poetic expression. Unfortunately, comparing also tends to make third borns jump to conclusions rather than use an ordered way of reasoning.

Third borns use humor as well as ideas to establish safe distance between themselves and others. Humor has the effect of creating just the right distance, not too close but not too far away, either. Thus, humor permits third borns to remain comfortable in otherwise emotionally threatening social settings. Unfortunately, third borns sometimes use humor inappropriately to the embarrassment of friends or family. Family members commonly complain third borns cannot ever be serious. Others are sometimes offended by the comparisons made in humor by third borns.

Empathy

Third borns usually have empathy for persons they perceive as victims. They frequently relate well to children, the handicapped, the aged, the poor, the outcasts, and so on. Perhaps they identify with them, or perhaps they find victims "safe" people with whom to associate. Perhaps it is some of both.

The empathy for victims sometimes leads third borns to choose unsavory companions as friends. Their parents have tried to get them to make better choices, often to no avail. The third born children prefer friends who feel nonthreatening to them rather than the friends their parents would select for them. Furthermore, third borns often find satisfaction as they see themselves helping these friends.

Empathy often encourages third borns to be rescuers. They not only befriend the less fortunate among their acquaintances, they also bring home lost kittens, care for baby birds who have fallen from the nest and give tender loving care to the family pet. Sometimes, third borns even rescue broken things by bringing them home. Some adult third borns fill their living space with stuff rescued from discarded junk which they think can be fixed and used sometime. However, they usually collect things far more rapidly than they can be repaired and used.

Compassion combines with creative thinking to make the third born enjoy solving problems for others. This pleasure over solving problems constitutes another reason for third borns to be attracted to unsavory friends. Third borns see them as having problems which they can help solve.

Third borns tend to be rebellious, much more so than any of the other birth orders. When told to do something, they may feel the need to prove they are fearless by not doing what they are told. Even adult third borns react negatively to being told to do things.

Summary

The third born personality is built around the feeling of vulnerability. This feeling causes them to battle fear, to generate ideas and to use humor to avoid scary confrontation, and to choose emotionally safe companions. They identify with victims and try to rescue them.

"I'm sorry it didn't turn out better for you. It was a good idea."

HOW TO LOVE THE THIRD BORN

Interventions

You might find loving a third born difficult if you experience this child as constantly rebelling, keeping company with children of whom you disapprove, and frequently expressing anger. You probably find yourself more angry at this child than loving.

To love this child, you need to have empathy for him or her. Since this child may seem to be strong willed, you might think this child needs a strong hand from you rather than empathy. However, if you could see inside the child you would see a child who feels as if the whole world could get to him or her any time it chose. You would see a child who lives with an unpleasant feeling of vulnerability.

Furthermore, you would see a child who feels there is no justice for him or her in the world. He or she thinks that at any given moment someone is going to treat him or her unfairly and his or her only defense is to not let it bother him or her.

Consequently, one way to express love to a third born is to sympathize, when appropriate, by saying "I'm sorry things are the way they are for you". Of course, you must be sincere, because if your tone of voice betrays a lack of sympathy, the words offend rather than make the third born feel loved. Rather than convey caring, they add more pain to what he or she is already experiencing.

When you sincerely sympathize with your third born you make him or her feel safe with you. You create a sense of security which is essential for this child to feel loved. Given the comfort of security, the third born comes to feel loved.

Third borns might not express it but they suffer pain when overlooked by you in favor of the other children. Long after the incident they remember the pain of having been treated unfairly. One third born child expressed the feeling by saying "Why do I always get the leftover money?" In her view, the other children got preference over her and she got leftovers. For this reason, you may need to take special care to be fair to the third born.

The feelings mentioned above are common to all the birth orders. However, third borns are more sensitive to the lack of security and to slights than other children, they are less likely to express feelings so parents recognize them, and they are less likely to assert themselves to deal with the feelings. Parents need to be especially sensitive to their feelings about injustice because third borns hide them so well.

In addition to providing security and avoiding injustice, third born children can be stroked by paying attention to their ideas. Since third borns generate ideas as a kind of defense, they feel cared for when their ideas receive attention. On the other hand, they could feel threatened if their ideas are rejected.

To convey caring, it is not necessary to agree with every idea. Some ideas are impractical, dangerous, unworkable or simply nonsense. After listening to an idea, it is all right to reject it if necessary. If you have listened, the third born usually feels all right and comes up with new, improved versions rather than be offended. From time to time, third borns come up with good ideas which work and please others, thereby making them feel loved. They truly contribute creatively to our society.

Also, you can communicate love by asking a third born for ideas. However, do not use this as a technique for dealing with third born misbehavior as in "How shall we solve this problem of your behavior"? Rather than feeling cared for, a third born feels put down by that question. You must express sincere desire to hear a third born's ideas in order to help him or her to feel loved.

If you find a third born feels hurt because you rejected an idea without giving it a fair hearing, you can often remedy the situation by apologizing. Saying you are sorry you did not listen to the idea as soon as you are aware of rejecting it can ease the hurt. It is better to apologize than to try to justify not listening. Explaining how you just do not have time to listen all the time does not make the third born feel loved. After all, you deemed something or someone else more important than him or her. Only an apology helps make it right.

If you inconvenience a third born of any age, an apology usually works wonders unless, of course, you overdo it. For example, if you were late, could not give help when it was requested, could not lend what he or she wanted to borrow, an apology creates a feeling of being loved in the third born. Just make certain your apology is an apology. Saying "I didn't mean to keep you waiting" does not mean the same as "I'm sorry I kept you waiting".

If you command a third born to do something, you may trigger the rebel within that child. In reaction to your command he or she could become angry, refuse to do what you have ordered him or her to do, or seethe internally. On the other hand, asking a third born to do something works far better in evoking a positive response. Adding the word "Please" to your requests works wonders with a third born.

Acknowledging something is scary can also create a sense of security for a third born, even though he or she denies the fear. For example, by telling a third born who is anxious about giving a speech that you imagine it is scary for him or her, you not only communicate caring but you relieve some of the fear by calling attention to it. Feelings that are examined tend to diminish.

Telling your third born you want to be fair to him or her helps establish rapport with this child. For this child to hear you genuinely care that things be fair to him or her is like a breath of fresh air.

When you need to do it, you can confront a third born by saying "I'm disappointed by what you did". By so saying, you suggest that your third born victimized you, making him or her regret what he or she has done. After such a confrontation, a third born tends to withdraw to process what you have said and probably apologizes later in words or actions. One teenage third born got up early in the morning to clean her room after her father told her he was disappointed she did not clean it the day before.

Use this confrontation sparingly and only when you need to because it causes pain to the child. Furthermore, using it frequently decreases its effectiveness. Save it for major disappointments rather than trivial transgressions.

Affirmations

Since your third born child lacks a defense system, you can love your child by suggesting it is all right to stand up for him or herself. Subconsciously believing he or she cannot do it, your child protests he or she does not know how. However, rather than trying to tell your child how he or she can be assertive, just assure the child there is a part of him or her which knows how to do it. This enables the child to draw on inner resources to be assertive instead of trying to be assertive in ways which do not suit his or her personality.

When encouraging your child to be assertive, be sure you give permission rather than telling him or her to do it because telling prompts the child to be aggressive instead of assertive. For example, permission says "It's okay for you to stand up for yourself." Commanding says "Stand up for yourself and don't let people walk over you". Permission allows the child to be assertive, commanding encourages the child to be aggressive.

Permission to assert him or herself allows the third born freedom to deal with injustice as it is perpetrated on him or her. No longer does he or she have to play the role of a smiling victim, a martyr.

Sometimes, third borns are picked on by other children because they do not have internal permission to fight. Without the freedom to fight, third born children avoid possible confrontations by walking away from disagreements. Because withdrawal frustrates other children who want to work out differences, these children sometimes harass third borns to involve them in working out differences. Unfortunately, such harassment usually succeeds in provoking a fight rather than a mutual working out of problems.

You might hesitate to give your child permission to fight for fear you could encourage him or her to fight constantly, to get hurt, or to become a bully. However, rather than promoting fighting, giving your third born permission to fight allows the child to take the risks which enable him or her to work out differences with friends. In the end, the child who has permission to fight has more friends than the child who does not have permission. Furthermore, the child with permission to fight usually gets into fewer conflicts.

You can relieve the burden of fearfulness for your third born by suggesting it is all right to enjoy being afraid. If he or she resists the idea, you can tell him or her other children enjoy being scared while riding roller coasters, watching scary movies and telling ghost stories. Since a third born is afraid of being afraid, you may have to repeat this affirmation several times for it to be effective.

When third borns succeed in turning off fear, they often experience boredom because they lack the stimulation of low level fear. They cannot get excited because the active ingredient of excitement is fear. To overcome boredom and to enjoy excitement they need permission to enjoy fear.

New experiences are always a bit scary for everyone and therefore stimulating for those who enjoy fear. By enjoying fear your child is not only more stimulated, he or she can welcome more new experiences.

If you observe your child trying hard to keep a stiff upper lip rather than giving in to feelings, it is time to suggest it is okay to be human rather than trying to be strong. In trying to be strong, a third born takes an emotionally precarious position on a pedestal from which he or she may fall into a pit of emotional inferiority. By suggesting it is okay to be human, you invite your child to tap his or her real strength. Furthermore, by allowing him or herself to be human, you enable the child to also feel loved.

Third borns tend to avoid asking for what they want or, if they do ask, they ask tentatively because they feel vulnerable when they ask. For third borns to ask puts them into a position of weakness which they fear others can exploit. Consequently, third borns often do without rather than make their desires known.

You can help overcome this difficulty by telling your third born child it is okay to ask. Of course, when the child does ask it is important to respond appropriately because asking is a major emotional risk for the third born. If you show irritation, exasperation or sarcasm in response to the request, you confirm for your third born it is not safe to ask.

The rejection of ideas is another source of pain for third borns. You can assist your child feel better by assuring him or her it is all right to feel okay, even when ideas are rejected. However, give this permission positively by saying "It's okay to feel okay when your ideas are rejected" rather than saying "It doesn't do any good to feel bad. You might as well feel okay". This latter statement does not help a third born feel loved.

When your third born feels bad for having been treated unfairly, you can assure him or her it is all right to feel okay in spite of such treatment. Saying this allows the third born to step out of the victim role to handle him or herself adequately. However, again be sure you are giving permission rather than hinting your third born is being weak. For example, say "You don't have to feel bad if you don't want to. It's okay to feel okay" but do not say "You're always feeling bad, and it's not necessary".

Of course, taking action on behalf of your third born would be seen as an act of love on your part, unless it makes him or her appear weak. Listen to your third born to discover the potential impact of what you contemplate doing.

If your third born is fearful, he or she usually seeks assurance everything will be all right. He or she is trying to make life absolutely safe. Logically, since such assurance is not possible, you could not give it nor make your third born believe it if you did give it. To provide a feeling of security, it is better to admit the reality that anything which happens to human beings could happen to him or her and yourself, and you take your chances as human beings. You can tell him or her "There's no way to be sure everything is going to turn out exactly right. It's okay to take your chances rather than being anxious". Do not say, "That's life. You have to take your chances."

As a parent, you may be distressed by defiance in your third born. Since this rebelliousness comes from getting angry over being commanded to do something, you can suggest to him or her it is okay to enjoy being told what to do. Let your child know this is just the way some people communicate. He or she can feel angry when told to do things or decide it is okay to enjoy it. If he or she can enjoy it, he or she can feel better than if he or she got angry about it. In other words, the child does not need to take on the victim role at being ordered to do things.

Finally, third borns often bristle at being put down. It is a form of humor they do not comprehend because they feel hurt by it. For them to enjoy this common form of humor they need to know it is all right for them to enjoy being put down. You can suggest it is okay to enjoy being put down, and offer examples of how other children and adults enjoy that kind of humor. He or she may have trouble believing put-downs can be enjoyed, but he or she will probably be intrigued by the idea and think about it. If the child decides it is okay to enjoy being put down, he or she can escape the victim role when others try to joke at his or her expense.

You will get lots of resistance from your third born to these affirmations if they seem risky to him or her. However, as you use the affirmations, you may find your third born making beneficial changes. He or she might not tell you "That's a great idea, thank you" but rather reflect the changes in his or her behavior. His or her response to these affirmations will probably be cautious and tentative.

Even though you may be tempted, resist forcing the affirmations if it is not immediately apparent they are working. Keep sowing the seed and in due time the crop ripens, if you are patient. Eventually, these affirmations do their work.

Summary

To love your third born child, provide security for him or her. Stand by him or her, affirm your loyalty, and recognize the child's feeling of vulnerability. Furthermore, refrain from using threats, intimidation, and force which would challenge the child to prove he or she is fearless. Listen respectfully to ideas, be sensitive to painful experiences and give sympathy when needed. Use "Please" freely when asking the child to do things.

How to Love Your Children

THE FOURTH BORN PERSONALITY

The third born pushes the fourth child into becoming a fourth born psychologically when he or she tries to pass on feelings of vulnerability to this child. Since the third born perceives the fourth born to be already vulnerable by virtue of being younger, passing on the feeling of vulnerability means simply telling the fourth born he or she is not old enough, big enough, fast enough or strong enough to play with him or her and the older children. Thus, by making the fourth born feel unwanted by older siblings because of immaturity, the third born causes the fourth born to believe no one wants him or her because of immaturity. This perception of self lasts a lifetime.

Fourth borns may decide they will always be immature, or may try to overcome the feelings, or may do some of both. If they give in to the feelings of immaturity, they continue to behave as if they cannot grow up. When acting immature, they often elicit reactions from others who tell them "Why don't you grow up?"

Behind the feeling of immaturity is also the fourth born belief that no one trusts him or her because of his or her immaturity. He or she is not permitted the responsibilities assigned the other children. He or she is not granted the privileges they receive. He or she is not included in family discussions. Trust, therefore, becomes a problem for fourth borns. They feel no one trusts them, they cannot trust themselves and they do not trust others.

A fourth born child can develop several strategies for trying to overcome the feeling of immaturity. For example, seeing the older siblings doing things which would be difficult for him or her to do, the fourth born decides the way to be grown up is to do difficult things. Consequently, a fourth born may prefer hard tasks over easy ones and choose more difficult ways over easier ways of doing things.

Or, a fourth born may decide the way to be grown up is to not listen to him or herself. The child reasons "If I'm not okay because I'm not grown up, maybe if I don't listen to myself I'll be okay". Consequently, strange as it may seem, many a fourth born is unable to listen to him or herself in situations which he or she perceives to be threatening.

By not listening to themselves, fourth borns experience confusion because they are unable to process information. For example, fourth borns have walked out on counseling sessions in frustration saying "I can't take this". They fled to escape the confusion which developed from not being able to listen to themselves when challenged. In situations where they are unable to withdraw physically, they simply become unresponsive. Fourth borns often signal their confusion when questioned by shrugging their shoulders without saying anything.

Fourth borns may try to pass the confusion on to others by saying things which do not make sense, things which may be bizarre. Usually, fourth borns are well aware they are trying to confuse others and often succeed in creating confusion. For example, by acting confused, fourth borns can get others to explain unnecessarily, to defend themselves, and to interpret events for them. However, the confusion continues to the frustration of those who deal with the fourth born.

Along with not listening to themselves, fourth borns may not listen to others. Rather than listening, they think about what they plan to say next. Their unrelated response lets you know they had you tuned out as you were talking.

Furthermore, fourth borns tend to believe others do not listen to them. They may try to force others to listen by talking loudly, or to shock people into listening by using profanity, or to talk fast to keep others listening once they start listening.

However, if nothing works, fourth borns may give up trying to communicate to others. In such cases they may simply stop talking, talk so softly they cannot be heard, or respond by saying "Forget it" if the other person does not hear the first time they speak.

None of the strategies fourth borns adopt succeed in overcoming the feeling of immaturity. Consequently, fourth borns tend to believe that, unless they are careful, others will always have the upper hand. In order to prevent this, fourth borns sometimes become bullies by beating up on other children in order to maintain an upper hand. Even as adults, fourth borns are sometimes abusive to spouses and/or children to keep them from having the upper hand. In fact, among the birth orders, fourth born men are the most likely to physically abuse their wives.

Strangely enough, your fourth born may not be able to have fun appropriately because he or she is unable to feel grown-up. On the one hand, he or she avoids looking immature by playing, and on the other, because of feeling immature he or she is unable to distinguish between when to play and when not to play. In other words, fourth borns who try to be mature cannot play and those who have given up trying to be mature cannot stop playing.

Feeling Excluded

Feeling no one wants them, fourth borns may simply exclude themselves from groups to defend against rejection. For example, in family gatherings they may be off alone rather than with the family members, or they may be playing with children rather than talking with adults. They may even withdraw from one-to-one relationships. One salesman reported that during their conversation the fourth born male client got down on the floor to play with the children while telling the salesman to "Keep talking; I'm listening".

Sometimes, instead of withdrawing, fourth borns take center stage to entertain everyone. They grab everyone's attention as they spout catchy one-liners, make humorous off-the-wall remarks, and put new twists on old ideas. The "life of the party" fourth borns appear entirely different from the shy wall-flowers who withdraw to be alone or to play with the children, but they both operate from the same subconscious motivations. The fourth born comedians also feel unwanted but have decided that if they can make people laugh, perhaps they will win acceptance. Fourth borns who have withdrawn feel defeated but those who entertain feel they are conquering the problem.

A fourth born may not want a friend to have friends for fear of being left out. He or she may try to encourage the friend to sever ties with other friends by finding fault with them. Frequently, when a fourth born marries, he or she may want the spouse to drop friends, limit contact with family, and spend most of the time at home. For example, one fourth born husband forbade his wife to have any contact with her parents or siblings unless he was present. Another would pester his wife whenever she was on the telephone, wanting to know to whom she was speaking or asking questions to interrupt the conversation. Fearful of being left out, the fourth born does not want his or her spouse to pay attention to anyone else.

Fourth Born Thinking

Perhaps because they are afraid people will not listen, fourth borns develop an analytical pattern of thinking. They constantly analyze events, persons, and ideas from every angle. They prepare for the future by analyzing. For example, if they anticipate an encounter with someone they think about every thing they could say to the person and about the various responses which the person might make. Out of all the possibilities, they choose what they say to the other person.

Because a fourth born constantly analyzes, he or she never makes a final decision. Every decision is subject to further analysis which may result in a change. In fact, much of what a fourth born says is introductory rather than conclusive. There is always something more to be said. This fourth born behavior can be especially frustrating to a spouse or child who relies on what the fourth born says as if it were a promise.

A fourth born often tries to hide ignorance for fear ignorance makes him or her look immature to others. To avoid appearing ignorant, he or she uses analyzing as a way to appear knowledgeable. However, analyzing limits a fourth born because it takes the place of learning new information. The fourth born realizes that learning something reveals a previous state of ignorance. For example, during counseling, a fourth born often claims to know what to do rather than admitting the need to learn something. Unfortunately, by being unwilling to learn, a fourth born actually causes others to regard him or her as intentionally ignorant.

In counseling, a fourth born may simply ask for a list of changes to make rather than information in order to solve a particular problem such as a marital crisis. He or she does not perceive learning as part of the solution. If he or she does want learn something, he or she often tries to do it secretly through someone else. For example, a fourth born may ask the spouse to relay information to him or her rather than going for counseling. By so doing, he or she hopes to hide any possible ignorance from the counselor.

Fourth borns also tend to be secretive, even with people closest to them, in order to keep others from having the upper hand. They hide their strategies, keep their thoughts to themselves and mislead others to keep them from guessing their intentions.

For example, a fourth born child may share with parents an elaborate, plausible, and detailed proposal of what he or she plans to do in order to cover up what he or she really intends to do. Because he or she gives so much detail, parents are apt to believe what he or she is saying instead of guessing what he or she actually has in mind. Also, in accounting for misbehavior, a fourth born child can give a detailed but false explanation of what took place. By thinking analytically, he or she can create the necessary detail to convincingly cover up his or her culpability.

Feeling Used

Fourth borns were often "used" as children. They felt used when older siblings asked them to do something, like get a ball, without including them in the game. Even though they became frustrated at being rejected despite the favor they had done, they could never refuse to do these favors when asked because of the hope of being included next time.

Subconsciously expecting to be used, fourth borns often react negatively to being asked to do something. However, they cannot refuse to do what is asked. Instead they tend to procrastinate, to get upset, or to do the task poorly. Ask them to get something, and they forget. Ask them to close the door, and they slam it. Ask them to vacuum the carpet, and they knock a plant off the end table. These fourth borns, expecting to be "used", act out of passive resistance.

A fourth born may use a defense system of "not caring" to deal with difficulties. For example, one fourth born high school student decided, in the middle of his senior year, he did not care about graduating. Things had become difficult for him and rather than telling himself he only had a few months to go, he told himself he did not care. Later, he regretted the decision but at the time it made sense to him to not care.

Fourth borns choose to not care because they perceive problems to be insurmountable. From their feelings of immaturity they do not expect to be able to solve problems so they hide behind a facade of not caring. At other times they simply deny that a problem exists rather than face it. For example, an abusive fourth born man may ask his wife to "forget about the past" rather than deal with the causes of his abusiveness.

Fourth borns tend to be very sensitive to blame and usually try to transfer the blame to someone or something else. Other children will do this also but not with the persistence of fourth borns. Even when faced with irrefutable evidence of their responsibility, they simply deny their culpability. By steadfastly claiming innocence, fourth borns sometimes succeed in getting others to believe them despite evidence to the contrary. If the evidence is simply another's word against their's, they are apt to convince others by their analytical creativity their word is the truth.

Sense of Justice

A fourth born tends to perceive justice as retaliatory, as getting even. When hurt by someone, he or she feels it is right to pay them back. For this reason, a fourth born man is the most likely to physically abuse his wife. For example, one man who must have been a fourth born asked a radio talk show host "Isn't it okay for me to hit my wife if she has had an affair?"

This tendency to hit probably rises from a wish the fourth born had as a child to be able to hit back when siblings hit him or her. The opportunity to get even presents itself when playing with neighborhood children or in adult life while living with family. In these situations the fourth born can become a bully.

Summary

In summary, fourth borns suffer from the twin problems of never feeling grown-up and of believing no one wants them. Trying to feel grown up, they tackle difficult challenges, choose not to listen to themselves and adopt an analytical way of thinking. Trying to deal with feeling unwanted, they either give in to the feelings by withdrawing or try to overcome them by entertaining everyone. They feel no one trusts them, they cannot trust themselves and they do not trust other people.

How to Love Your Children

"That was a difficult project. I'm proud you are my son."

HOW TO LOVE THE FOURTH BORN

Interventions

Your fourth born child is the most likely to come to you for affection. This child may enjoy hugs, sitting on your lap and holding your hand as you walk with him or her. It would seem the easiest to love this child since all you have to do is respond to the child's overtures. You may not realize it, but your fourth born comes for affection frequently because this child has come to believe no one wants him or her and is looking for reassurance of acceptance.

Even though the fourth born comes for attention, the fourth born is easy to overlook because he or she tends to fade into the background when competing with the older siblings. The other children push the fourth born aside as they are demanding attention. Feeling unwanted, the fourth born accepts this position as his or her lot in life.

How to Love Your Children

Even in adult life, the fourth born is often forgotten when important events occur. For example, in one family everyone except the fourth born was notified when the father was admitted to the hospital with a heart attack. Even after he learned his father was in the hospital, he was left out by his siblings when they discussed their father's treatment plans. However, they were not being malicious. They just forgot him.

A fourth born feels loved when included. For example, a woman got a credit card for herself but not one for her fourth born husband because she made all the family purchases. When he discovered she did not get him one as well, he felt hurt at being excluded. He cheered up when she told him he was included in the card she had gotten.

There are numerous ways to include the fourth born. You can use possessive expressions which express belonging by saying such things as "This is my son" or "This is my daughter". One woman told her fourth born husband "You are my husband" to his immense satisfaction. Other birth orders may feel smothered by such statements but a fourth born relishes them. He or she loves the assurance of belonging, the feeling of being wanted.

Similarly, the phrase "I want you" conveys love to your fourth born. The statement can be imbedded in a sentence such as "I want you to go with me to the mall" or "I want you here by me". The child will hear the "I want you" and feel loved. Of course, if you say it in anger it may create negative feelings instead of inducing a feeling of love.

You may be tempted to chide the fourth born for excluding him or herself but you would be making a mistake. For example, it hurts the child who has withdrawn for you to ask why he or she is all alone instead of with everyone else. It is more loving to invite him or her back saying "I want you to be with us".

Perhaps the simplest way to include persons is to hug them. Fourth borns usually like to be hugged, especially as children. As young children, they may come to you for hugs or give them to you spontaneously. Usually, the more you hug fourth borns, the more they feel included and loved.

Since fourth borns often court difficulty in order to prove themselves mature, offering difficult challenges tends to increase their self-esteem and feeling of being loved. For example, by insinuating "I don't know if you can but I would like for you to polish the brass", you offer a challenge fourth borns can hardly turn down. This type of challenge often works with adult fourth borns as well.

Asking a fourth born to do difficult tasks implies confidence in his or her maturity. In fact, suggesting the job is difficult usually brings a more positive response than just asking a fourth born to do a chore. For example, it is better to say to a fourth born "Do you think you can do the dishes? There are quite a few of them" rather than asking him or her "Would you do the dishes?"

Simple asking is onerous to fourth borns because they anticipate being used and they do not like it. When asked for a favor, they often think "I'm going to be used again". Consequently, when asking them to do something it is better to include a challenge about their ability to do the job.

On the other hand, suggesting a task is easy demotivates them. Fourth borns do not enjoy doing something which has been deemed easy because it suggests they are immature. Furthermore, what if they could not do the job after it had been called "easy"? They fear being embarrassed if they should be unable to do an "easy" chore. Consequently, a difficult task is more inviting to a fourth born than an easy task.

If you want a fourth born to accept what you say, suggest it may be difficult for him or her to believe what you are telling him or her. For example, you can say "This may be hard for you to believe, but we like to have you with us" or "This may be hard for you to believe, but I will not tolerate that kind of behavior". A fourth born just about has to believe something when it may be hard to believe.

Similarly, you can get a fourth born's attention by saying "I have something to tell you which is very difficult for me to talk about". After hearing the reference to difficulty, a fourth born wants to hear what you have to say. Furthermore, the fourth born is going to be more open toward you than if you simply blurted out what you wanted to say. He or she wants to make it easy for you so he or she can be more grown up than you are.

Affirmations

Since fourth borns suffer from feeling immature, they need to hear it is okay to be grown up. By making positive statements such as "It's okay to be grown up" rather than critical statements such as "Quit being so childish", you

How to Love Your Children

give them permission to feel grown-up. You can remind them it is okay for them to be grown up when you see immaturity as an issue with them.

Sometimes, instead of acting immature, a fourth born acts super mature. He or she rejects immaturity by choosing to always be mature. In doing so, this fourth born makes it very difficult for him or her to enjoy life. He or she needs permission to enjoy being a child in order to play. For example, if your child seems obsessed with work while rejecting play, you can tell him or her "It's okay for you to have fun". To increase the likelihood the child will accept your suggestion, you can challenge him or her by saying "This may be hard for you to believe but it is okay for you to have fun". It is also helpful to a fourth born if you tell him or her adults have fun, too.

If your fourth born is obsessed with doing things the most difficult way, you can assure him or her it is okay to do things the easy way as long as they are done right. You can strengthen your affirmation by explaining that the more mature a person becomes, the easier things become for him or her. In other words, as you gain experience by maturing you can do things more easily. This perception allows your child to enjoy being grown up rather than always having to court difficulty in order to try to feel grown up.

When a fourth born gets confused, he or she is probably not listening to him or herself. You can help clear up the confusion by telling him or her "It is okay for you to listen to yourself". Because shrugs are a sign of this confusion, you can use them as cue to give this permission to listen to self. This permission statement may sound strange to you but it makes sense to a fourth born.

If your fourth born does not understand listening to self, you can explain that when he or she thinks something or says something he or she can listen to it. If the child says he or she does not know how to do that, assure the child a part of him or her does know how to listen to self.

A fourth born tends to feel bad when others do not listen. In order to deliver your fourth born from feeling victimized by this behavior, suggest that since feeling bad is not going to make others listen, it is okay to feel okay when they do not listen. Not only is he or she apt to feel better, but when feeling good he or she is more likely to also find effective ways to get others to pay attention. For example, a man who decided to feel okay when his boss did not listen found a successful way to make his boss listen. One day, when his boss his boss was shuffling papers instead of listening, he locked the office door, took his shoes off, climbed on the boss's desk, jumped up and down a few times, and then asked his boss if he would listen. After that, every time the boss would show signs of not listening, he would ask "Do I have to get up on your desk again?" Needless to say, his boss listened.

As a matter of fact, fourth borns do adopt various strategies for getting others to listen. Some fourth borns talk loudly to make themselves heard, others speak softly to force others to pay close attention, some wait to say anything until asked, and still others say outrageous things to get a hearing. However, since these strategies arise from feeling bad, they tend to be ineffective. Fourth borns who allow themselves to feel okay discover better ways of being heard.

Since everyone gets left out of things at times, fourth borns need to know it is all right to feel okay when they are omitted. This can be communicated to the child by telling him or her "You have been left out, but you do not have to feel bad if you don't want. It's all right to feel okay even though you have been left out." This affirmation may take a while to take root in the fourth born's thinking.

Fourth borns tend to accept being left out without resisting. It never occurs to them they might be able to do something to include themselves. Telling them "You can ask to take part even if you were not invited" opens up the possibility of seeking admittance to groups instead of withdrawing. When they include themselves they discover they are welcome in groups. They have been excluding themselves unnecessarily.

For example, instead of waiting till someone invites the fourth born child to play ball, the child can ask to play. Encouraging this child to approach groups helps overcome the belief which says "No one wants me". Asking to belong may be difficult at first but realizing it is difficult can motivate the fourth born to do it.

When blamed, you will notice fourth borns usually look for a way to shift the blame to someone else or at least off themselves. When you tell them it is not necessary to feel bad when blamed, you help them feel better and to accept responsibility for what they have done.

Along with sensitivity to blame, fourth borns practice psychological withdrawal in self defense. Physically, they withdraw with a shrug of the shoulders; emotionally, they decide they do not care. It is a tempting to try to force the fourth born to respond or to care. However, it is much like beating on the shell of a turtle to get it to stick out its head. Rather than yielding to the temptation it is better to affirm "It is okay for you to care". The child may not respond immediately, but the seed you have planted may bear fruit later.

Fourth borns grow up feeling they have no influence over how others feel. Their experience tells them everyone controls their own feelings without being affected by whatever the they do. Consequently, they can behave obnoxiously with no awareness of how this behavior influences others' feelings. Likewise, they often think they cannot do anything which would help others feel good. They need to understand their behavior does affect others' feelings and that it is all right to take responsibility for how others feel toward them.

Finally, a fourth born needs help with his or her feelings about being used. Not only does a fourth born feel badly about being used, he or she tends to feel in danger of being used when asked to do something. By suggesting it is not necessary to feel bad just because someone has taken advantage of him or her, you can help this child overcome the anger. In other words, tell this child it is all right to feel okay when he or she has been used.

Summary

A fourth born feels loved when allowed to feel grown up and when given a sense of belonging. You can help convey a feeling of maturity by giving the child difficult challenges. You can help convey a feeling of belonging by including him or her with "You belong to me" and by inviting him or her to participate.

PARENTING AS AN ONLY

If you are an only child, your parenting style is formed by your habit of thinking with your emotions, your need to control your circumstances and your perception of equality as justice.

As an only child, you relate to your children emotionally. You have feelings about what they do, good or bad. Because you think with your emotions, you tend to react rather than interact with them. For example, when they ask for something, your first response is apt to be "No" after which you start thinking about whether it might be okay to allow their request.

As an only, you tend to project expectations on your children. If your child does not behave as you anticipate, you become frustrated. For example, you might expect your child to be reasonable if you explain things to him or her. However, a child may see explanations as something with which to argue rather than to accept. In fact, the more explanations a child receives, the more obnoxious he or she could become. Sometimes, it becomes necessary for the only child parent to simply claim parental authority by saying "Because I said so" rather than explaining.

Only children, as parents, try to understand children (and others) by imagining themselves in their place rather than listening to them. Consequently, they understand only child behavior but not that of the other birth orders. These parents can become frustrated with their children of other birth orders, saying things like "I just don't understand you" or "I just don't know why you do things the way you do". If you find yourself depicted here, realize understanding comes by listening to your children, not by projecting yourself into their situations.

How to Love Your Children

Because your sense of justice is based on treating everyone alike, you tend to try to give equal treatment to each of our children. If you do something for one child, you also try to do the same for each child. For example, when giving holiday gifts, you would see to it each child got the same number of packages with the same dollar value. Even when buying birthday gifts, you might buy for every child rather than just for the birthday child.

Furthermore, if you are in charge of opening gifts, you probably see to it they are opened one at a time so everyone has a chance to watch, to admire each gift, and to take pictures. By so organizing the opening of gifts, you make sure each child gets the same attention rather than making each child fend for him or herself.

Disliking intrusion yourself, you do not want to pressure your children. Consequently, as an only child parent you tend to explain rather than command, to do things yourself rather than require your children to do them, and to adjust to your children rather than require them to adjust to you.

However, even though you make life easy for your children, they do not become dependent on you for life. Rather, they learn from the positive example you set to practice the same kinds of behavior in their adult lives. In other words, you teach by modeling ambition for your children rather than by requiring your children to work.

Since you want to escape intrusive suggestions from others by parenting correctly, your biggest parenting handicap is probably expressed by the word "Should". You have learned, from whatever source, how children "should" behave and you want to make sure your children behave that way. Rather than trusting your own parenting instincts which take into consideration various circumstances, you probably try to make your children fit a mold and become frustrated when they do not. Your children, in turn, become frustrated at not being able to be themselves.

As an only child, you tend to feel bad when your child feels bad. Consequently, in order to make yourself feel better when your child feels bad, you try to make him or her feel better quickly rather than taking time to listen. You either try to fix the problem immediately or tell the child he or she should not feel bad because the problem cannot be fixed. For example, when your child comes home angry, you tend to ask "What's the matter?" in order to discover what you can fix rather than allowing the child to vent his or her feelings. It would be better to respond to his or her feelings by saying "You really sound angry" rather than demanding information.

By responding to the non-verbal communication of feelings you establish rapport with your child. Furthermore, when you respond to feelings, you make it easier for him or her to tell you what the problem is. For example, your child might tell you "Yes, I'm angry! That mean kid next door threw my pencil out the school window."

As an only, you tend to bring feelings home from work and interact with family as you would like to interact with people on the job. In other words, if you feel angry at work, you express anger at home to family members. If you do bring feelings home, you need to find ways to leave bad feelings on the job rather than inflicting them on family. Likewise, you need to leave feelings at home when you go to work.

You probably crave time to relax when you first get home from work. You would like to have a half hour to be alone without having to interact with anyone. This urge probably conflicts with the needs of the children to interact with you as soon as you walk in the door. For your children's sake, you need to be aware of this tendency and make arrangements to relax without expecting children to stand by while you take the time to unwind.

Raising an Only:

If your child is an only child, conflicts between the two of you can escalate because you both react to each other. For example, if the child asks to go outside, you automatically say "No", your child reacts angrily to the denial, and you react angrily to the child's anger, and so on.

In order to overcome the conflict, you need to listen to the child. When your child has a tantrum, you need to allow yourself to stay calm rather than escalating the conflict. By modeling the kind of behavior you want from your child, you can help induce changes in your child's behavior. To do this, realize you can be firm without having to be emotional. However, if the child has been using tantrums for a time, it takes patience to bring about change.

Raising a First Born:

In relating to your first born child, you would like to help promote his or her goals. However, when you try to

How to Love Your Children

help your child, you may become frustrated because he or she is fickle with goals. Just as you are helping him or her toward a particular goal, you discover your first born has changed interests. In order to be comfortable with helping a first born, you must remember first born goals are actually dreams which he or she changes easily.

However, you may be even more frustrated with your first born's disorganization. He or she does not have a place for everything nor everything in its place. He or she does not adhere to a schedule. He or she changes plans at a moment's notice when friends want him or her to do something. You do not like these behaviors but you only experience frustration if you try to organize him or her. For your sake and the sake of your child, you need to develop patience with the disorganization of your first born.

Raising a Second Born:

As for the second born, you probably get along well with this child. He or she is usually dependable and accepts controls. In fact, this child probably demonstrates self- discipline which enables him or her to get things done, which allows him or her to resist peer pressure, and which prompts him or her to make good choices. While these behaviors make you comfortable, your second born lacks means of coping with your expressions of feeling. He or she probably avoids facing your feelings by not informing you about many things. As an only, you need to shift into your rational mode to communicate with your second born.

Raising a Third Born:

You could be the least comfortable with the third born child. You worry about his or her reckless behavior if he or she is fearless, or you worry about his or her tendency to not get involved if he or she is the fearful type. If you try to change your third born's behavior, you find you lack the strategies to do so. To reach your third born, you need to be able to give sympathetic attention rather than trying to fix things.

Raising a Fourth Born:

You would probably have the least conflict with the fourth born who tends to withdraw rather than be open. Since this child tends to clam up, you can project your ideas on him or her without getting much resistance. In fact, the fourth born is apt to believe what you say about him or her rather than denying it. From his or her position of felt immaturity, the fourth born probably assumes you know more about him or her than he or she knows about him or herself. To deal with this child, you need to listen carefully rather than trying to make the child conform to what you think.

Parenting in Partnership

As an only child parent, you tend to parent individually rather than cooperatively with your spouse. In some situations you defer to your spouse and in other situations handle them yourself. For example, an only child mother may become frustrated at dealing with the children and appeal to her husband saying "You handle it. I can't take it any more." In other words, as an only you either parent on your own or you expect your partner to take over. It is not a cooperative effort.

Parenting with an Only:

When married to another only, you are especially prone to parenting individually rather than working together. The two of you do not intrude on each other because you tend to think alike. Two onlies, married to each other, tend not to pressure or to feel pressured by each other, as opposed to being married to someone of another birth order. Their interactions are such they do not interfere with each other. However, both tend to live in their own private worlds.

In this family, children tend to recognize their parents' moods and learn to not intrude on them. They realize their parents react emotionally and tend to avoid topics which would trigger the reactions.

Parenting with a First Born:

If you are an only married to a first born, you could be carrying more than your share of the parenting burden, especially if you are the mother. Your spouse would tend to demand respect of the children in the form of instant obedience while ignoring their needs, desires and feelings. In order to prevent pressure by your first born spouse, you might do the parenting except when the children get out of hand. Then you might say "Wait till your father gets home", knowing the children are afraid of their father.

How to Love Your Children

If you are the father, you might be frustrated by the chaos created by your first born wife. Decisions are made at the last minute, changes take place with no notice, and agreements are forgotten. Your home does not have the order you crave. Your children probably appeal to you for relief from your wife's demands for respect.

Parenting with a Second Born:

If you are married to a second born, you tend to supply the emotional side of parenting while your spouse deals with the children rationally. Generally, a second born defers to an only child parent because parenting requires attention to feelings, and the only is more comfortable with feelings than is the second born. However, the rational, cut-and-dried disciplinary methods of the second born may be uncomfortable to you. You may wish he or she would pay more attention to feelings.

Parenting with a Third Born:

If you are married to a third born, you probably have some difficulty with your spouse's spontaneity. The two of you may disagree on parenting styles: you wanting to organize the children and your spouse wanting to give them more freedom. Also, your spouse may feel a need to protect the children from your anger, especially if you are the husband. Consequently, you may get angry over having your parenting style corrected in addition to being angry at the children's behavior. Your children tend to ignore you because they can retreat to your spouse who "protects" them from you. You and your spouse need to comprehend each other's personalities, parenting styles, and concerns, in order to harmonize your parenting.

Your spouse may have a disconcerting effect of asking you "Why" questions. For example, he or she may ask why you do not listen to your daughter, why you try to force the children to do things, or why you are so emotional. You probably find these kinds of questions highly intrusive because they imply corrective criticism. You need to allow yourself to feel okay despite the questions.

Parenting with a Fourth Born:

Parenting while married to a fourth born may cause you great difficulty. Your spouse's tendency to choose a favorite among the children violates your sense of justice. Furthermore, your spouse may demand more of your first born child than seems reasonable to you. In addition, you may be burdened by your spouse's unrealistic expectations of how you should be able to discipline, control, or guide your children effortlessly. It may seem to you, with some justification, the parenting responsibility is largely yours.

You may be especially frustrated when your spouse becomes a playmate to your children, as fourth borns are apt to do. While you are trying to maintain order, your spouse creates difficulty by acting like one of the children. For example, you may want to get your children to bed but your partner may let the children stay up as late as they wish without regard to how tired they will be in the morning.

Summary

Regardless of the birth order of your spouse, you tend to be a responsible parent who keeps order in the family. You bring emotion to the task: rejoicing when there is cause to rejoice and getting upset when there is cause to be upset. However, despite your emotional nature, your children probably do not experience the pressure they would get from other birth order parents.

How to Love Your Children

PARENTING AS A FIRST BORN

If you are a first born parent, you are likely to love conditionally. Therefore, rather than truly loving your children, you demand respect from them. You look for instant obedience, complete agreement, and a compliant attitude as signs they respect you. You are prepared to be angry if respect is not forthcoming.

You want your children to be exemplary so others think well of you as a parent. You value their good behavior in public and you take it as a personal affront if they misbehave. You are pleased when you can take pride in them. You might get a lump in your throat or a tear in your eye when they perform well, especially if someone praises them to you.

Psychologically, a major problem for you in parenting is you do not understand anyone on a gut level. During childhood, when you should have been learning about personalities, you felt no need to do it. As the oldest child, you did not have to understand your younger siblings because you could dominate them. To get along, the younger children had to figure you out but you did not have to figure them out. Consequently, even as an adult, others can see through you but to you they are opaque.

Your challenge as a parent is to understand your children so you can use other strategies to deal with them rather than forcing them to render your respect. Because you need to understand your children, you will find this book to be especially important to you. Perhaps through this book you can experience the joy of creating a love relationship with your children.

Raising an Only:

If you parent an only child, your demand for respect through immediate obedience intrudes on this child's internal schedule. The child is not ready to drop what he or she is doing to fulfill your demands. He or she needs time to adjust to the change. Consequently, your only child may react strongly when you expect instant obedience. If your marriage partner is strong enough to intervene, you could be forced to give the only child leeway. Nevertheless, you seethe inside at being unable to require respect. However, your only child is more comfortable at not having to respond instantly.

You can also be more comfortable, if you realize the only child operates on an internal schedule which is difficult to set aside. When you recognize this only child characteristic, you can be more at ease with his or her behavior. However, if you continue to demand this child adjust to you rather than taking his or her mental schedule into consideration, you make life miserable for him or her. You need to value love over respect in order to be a loving parent.

Raising a First Born:

As a first born, you may have conflict with your first born child over who is going to demand respect from whom. The conflict creates a power struggle between yourself and him or her. This child demands to do things which you do not want him or her to do, simply for the respect. For example, your first born son might ask to go downtown with friends, expecting you to "respect" his right to do so. You may not realize it, but your son's desire to go downtown could be to prove to his friends you respect him enough to let him go.

In seeking respect, your first born may also be trying subconsciously to "prove" you do not love him or her, thus confirming his or her view the world is without love for him or her. Consequently, by establishing you are forbidding a particular behavior which he or she thinks is all right, he or she can nurse resentments over being "Unloved". Your demand for respect plays into the first born's loveless script.

Raising a Second Born:

As a first born parent, you probably have less conflict with a second born child. This child has learned to adjust to first borns by having to deal with an older first born sibling, and he or she uses this skill to deal with you. Consequently, rather than getting into a power struggle with you, this child knows how to manipulate you to get what he or she wants. At times, his or her logic may draw respect from you rather than enabling you to demand respect from him or her.

Raising a Third Born:

Your greatest conflict will probably be with your third born child, especially if he or she is of the fearless type. Thus, if you try to demand respect by threatening the child with consequences, by requiring unquestioning obedience of the child, or by issuing ultimatums to the child, the child could feel compelled to "prove" he or she is not afraid of you. This rebellion can reach traumatic proportions, if you demand respect forcefully enough long enough and your child resists fearlessly enough.

On the other hand, you would have little conflict with a fearful third born who would tend to cave in to any threat. This child tends to be intimidated by your demands for respect and does nothing which would invite your wrath.

Raising a Fourth Born:

You probably have less difficulty with the fourth born who is able to frustrate you but usually does not defy you. Your demands for respect from this child will often be thwarted by this child bringing up technicalities, pleading ignorance or claiming not to have understood what you were saying. The fourth born appears compliant but never really does exactly what you want. You do not have the strategies from your experience as a first born to deal with this behavior.

Parenting in Partnership

Parenting with an Only:

If you are married to an only child, your spouse probably keeps you from fully exerting your demands for respect. For example, your spouse understands the need for your children to have lead time rather than having to act immediately when you demand it. Furthermore, an only child spouse probably encourages the children to go along with you in order to preserve peace, thereby reducing the need for you to demand respect.

You may try to support your only child spouse by demanding respect from the children on his or her behalf. Your spouse appears to need help because of his or her tendency to argue ineffectively with the children. However, he or she probably does not appreciate your efforts at strengthening his or her hand. Rather, he or she tends to see your actions as intrusive rather than supportive.

Parenting with a First Born:

Married to another first born, you may both demand respect from your children. Your children may experience your authority as overpowering and adjust to it, except possibly for your fearless third born. On the positive side, both of you will try to encourage your children by emphasizing long range goals for them to pursue. To your discouragement, apart from your first born, none of your children buy into these goals.

Parenting with a Second Born:

If you are married to a second born, your spouse usually has the upper hand. He or she is more decisive, clearcut and logical than you in dealing with the children. Also, since your spouse is probably able to put you in your place with a look or a comment, you may defer to him or her in dealing with the children.

You may find your second born spouse objects to your praising the first born as he or she tries to protect the second born from feeling inadequate. You may feel stymied unless you understand your spouse is trying to protect the second child rather than just being unfair to the oldest child.

Parenting with a Third Born:

If you are married to a third born, your spouse may have the upper hand if he or she is fearless, or may be dependent on you if he or she is fearful. If fearless, your spouse may have such control over you you capitulate to him or her. Your spouse calls the shots and you walk gingerly around him or her. If fearful, your spouse appears so fragile you walk on egg shells for fear of causing him or her to break. Either way, you are probably unable to demand respect at home.

Parenting as a First Born

Parenting with a Fourth Born:

You will probably have a compatible relationship in being married to a fourth born, inasmuch as he or she probably does not challenge your tendency to demand respect. This marriage works well for the children because you may not feel as much need to demand respect of your children since you get it from your spouse. Furthermore, your spouse may not be as inclined to come down hard on the children, especially the first born, because to do so might trigger your wrath.

Summary

In general, to parent adequately as a first born you need to value love over respect. You can gain the respect you want better by loving the children rather than by demanding respect from them.

You are able to be strong with your children. This strength becomes an asset when it is tempered with love.

How to Love Your Children

PARENTING AS A SECOND BORN

As a second born parent, you tend to ignore feelings in dealing with people, including family. Family is important to you but you might not think about your children's feelings or connect with them emotionally. For example, you may apply rules arbitrarily rather than respond sensitively to the emotional needs of your children.

Insensitive to feelings, you may not realize the impact a statement can have. A statement, frequently made by second born parents to their children, is worth repeating here because it causes many problems for children as they grow up. The statement is made when a child has gotten him or herself into an uncomfortable situation. The statement says "You made your bed, so you lie in it".

The statement is meant to make children think of consequences when they launch on a project, take on a commitment or make an investment of time, money or effort. However, the statement does not cause children to make better commitments but causes them to fear making commitments. Carried into adulthood, this fear of making commitments forces many to go from job to job or from marriage to marriage. Some are unable to take jobs or get married for fear of being trapped.

When people who fear committing themselves try to make commitments, they keep an escape route open. They never fully give themselves to a job or get fully involved in a marriage. For example, they start looking for a new job as soon as they take a job, and they keep outside relationships alive which interfere with their marital relationships.

Sometimes, they keep themselves unhappy in the belief that feeling bad allows them the option of leaving the commitment. If they allow themselves to be happy, they feel they might become trapped in the commitment.

Children need to be given the option of changing their minds once they have made a commitment. Otherwise, they cannot take the risk of making commitments as children or as adults. A child needs permission to remake the bed rather than being forced to "lie in it".

As a second born, you can improve your parenting by becoming aware of the feelings of your children. You can start by allowing yourself to have feelings and to pay attention to them. Think about how you feel and about how your children feel.

Raising an Only:

Because an only child dislikes the corrections you like to give, he or she may simply withdraw into his or her own world to escape. If you express your caring for this child by suggesting ways to improve on good performance, your constructive criticism is an unwanted intrusion into his or her life. Since this child tends to retreat into his or her own world anyway, he or she might do it more intensely to escape feeling bad. As a result, this child may not share much with you.

This child's emotional reactions can be aggravating to you. You want to lead your child into thinking rationally but without effect. Despite your efforts, your only child remains emotional.

Raising a First Born:

As a second born, you tend to withhold compliments, praise and approval from your children, especially from the first born. You feel the need to protect your children from being made to feel inadequate as you were made to feel inadequate when you were outdone by your first born sibling. Consequently, by keeping the first born from glorying in his or her accomplishments, you hope to shield the second born from pain of being compared unfavorably to him or her. However, you tend to withhold compliments not only from the first born but from all the children.

Consequently, by not getting positive feedback from you, your first born child can become discouraged. If your first born is of the opposite sex to you, he or she might become depressed because his or her anger turns inward. If he or she is of the same sex, he or she is more likely to become angry at you. Your first born may give up trying because he or she anticipates your criticizing him or her rather than giving approval.

You tend to give suggestions for improvement as an expression of your love, especially when a child does well at something. You yourself appreciate suggestions which help you toward perfection, and so does your second born child, but your first born feels discouraged at never being able to get your unqualified approval.

Raising a Second Born:

Your second born child could do well as you offer him or her suggestions for improvement. However, he or she may have trouble with feelings, not only because he or she is a second born but because you respond logically rather than emotionally. If you and your spouse are both second born, your combined characteristics can cause the child to have great difficulty with feelings.

Raising a Third Born:

If your child is third born, he or she may frustrate you by disagreeing with your judgments. This child will want to give everyone the benefit of the doubt, defend everyone and refuse to say bad things about anyone. Furthermore, this child will tend to jump to conclusions rather than think things through, a behavior which is contrary to your ways of thinking. Consequently, the third born child will probably make you uncomfortable and you might feel helpless in dealing with this child.

Your third born child has learned from early on how to deal with second borns through coping with the second born sibling harassing him or her. The skills developed in that relationship transfer to this child's interaction with you, giving him or her a psychological advantage over you. Because you do not understand this child, you could find yourself using force in dealing with him or her.

Raising a Fourth Born:

Your fourth born child's logic may keep you off balance. Before saying something, this child tends to analyze things thoroughly and is often able to manipulate you into thinking his or her way. If this child is unable to influence you one time, the next time he or she will have figured out something new to try. Because you omit the emotional content of thought, you may not be able to see through what your child is saying. For example, your child may explain in detail why he needs to go to the library, all the while planning to do something of which you would not approve if you knew. But because of all the logical detail he or she provides, he or she convinces you.

Parenting in Partnership

Parenting with an Only:

If you are married to an only, your spouse tends to balance your rational tendencies with his or her emotional tendencies. Together, you provide a healthy balance for the children. However, if you insist parenting be done your way, you could create feelings of resentment in your spouse as well as impose your rational ways on the children. Although your spouse might try to emulate your ways because of wanting to do things right, he or she may become depressed rather than accomplishing the feat of becoming rational rather than emotional.

Parenting with a First Born:

If you are married to a first born, you have the upper hand, psychologically. You learned early in childhood how to deal with a first born and you know instinctively how to get through to him or her. The first born has no defense to your strategies, even when you do not consciously try to make him or her uncomfortable. In fact, a first born is probably more on guard than relaxed in your presence. Sensitive to disagreement, the first born constantly anticipates you are going to disagree with what he or she says.

Marriage between second borns and first borns is fairly uncommon because of the discomfort first borns feel with second borns. It is more likely to happen if the first born had a second born parent of the same sex with whom he or she had a good relationship.

You could be frustrated with the first born because of his or her tendency to color circumstances to make him or herself look good. Since this appears dishonest to you, you tend to get angry at this behavior. However, your spouse might not change but may try harder to be more skillful at lying so as to not be detected next time.

Just as the first born used force on the second born during childhood, your first born spouse may try to force you to conform to him or her. While he or she could use physical force, he or she is more apt to use emotional, psychological, or financial force, often in the form of an ultimatum. For example, your spouse may tell you unless you do what he or she wants, he or she will quit work.

Married to each other, a second born and a first born need to pay special attention to creating a good relationship between themselves in order to provide a healthy home for their children.

Parenting with a Second Born:

If you are married to a second born, you need to pay special attention to your children's feelings because your natural tendencies are reinforced by your spouse. With both of you as second borns, your children may have little emotional contact with either of you. Phrases such as "That's not necessary" and "You don't need to do that" are indicators you and/or your spouse are rejecting feelings. These phrases suggest necessity, rather than emotion, determines behaviors. These phrases are disheartening to your children.

Parenting with a Third Born:

If you are married to a third born, your spouse has the psychological advantage. He or she has learned to deal with second borns from childhood and instinctively knows how to get to you. Your instinct is to use force which will backfire if your spouse is a fearless type third born.

In this marriage, you try to control the children and your spouse tries to nurture them, which can be a healthy balance. However, your spouse may interfere with your control, frustrating you and encouraging the children to ignore your authority. This can lead children to defy all authority. If your children are getting into trouble with authority outside the home, you and your spouse need to reach an agreement in which he or she does not interfere with your exercising control and you are reasonable with your children. By so doing, the two of you can teach your children to respect authority.

Parenting with a Fourth Born:

If you are married to a fourth born, you may be manipulated by him or her. You are unable to argue successfully with him or her because of the leaps in logic he or she makes. You reason by limiting propositions; your spouse

How to Love Your Children

reasons by introducing new propositions. Consequently, you could find yourself constantly being confused by your spouse and becoming cautious in reasoning with him or her.

Your fourth born spouse may be emotionally closer to the children because he or she is able to relate to them on their level. Therefore, your spouse is liable to side with the children when you want to exercise discipline, frustrating you by rendering your discipline ineffective.

However, if there is conflict between your fourth born spouse and the children, you are apt to side with your spouse. Your spouse can probably persuade you that if the children would just do what he or she wants, then everything would be all right. Given that belief, you are likely to require the children to adjust to your spouse rather than asking your spouse change his or her ways. Consequently, if your spouse is unreasonable, this unfair scenario can generate deep anger or frustration in your children. For their sake, it may be necessary for you to think about how the children feel rather than simply try to maintain peace.

Summary

Finally, to be a better parent you need to consider feelings by allowing them in yourself and by thinking about how your children feel. Your strengths in parenting lie in your self-discipline, your ability to think logically, and your ability to do whatever is necessary to solve problems.

PARENTING AS A THIRD BORN

If you are a third born parent, you are probably full of compassion for your children. You want them to feel loved, to be protected, and to have plenty of your attention. However, because you feel such compassion you may find parenting to be an all consuming task from which you have no respite.

Believe it or not, because third born mothers take parenting so seriously, they are the most likely to allow the father to have the children in a divorce if they believe he is capable of caring for them. They love their children but leave them to their father to escape the difficult job of parenting.

As a third born parent, you give rather than receive. Your relationship with your children focuses on their needs rather than your own. You exist entirely for your children rather than expecting them to exist for you. Your greatest disappointment would be if your children felt unloved by you.

However, in dealing with your children you want to make them feel loved rather than simply loving them. The difference is this: in making them feel loved, you impose your thoughts on them whereas in loving them, you would tune into their thoughts. For example, in making your children feel loved you decide to have them cut out paper dolls because it is raining outside; in loving them you find out what they would like to do and help them do it, even if they want to spend time alone rather than with you.

Raising an Only:

If you are the parent of an only child, you probably get along well with the child. While you do offer suggestions, your presence may not feel intrusive to the child. Furthermore, you would tend to not apply pressure so your child would feel the need to fight for space or time.

The problems with an only child would arise from your spontaneity which might make your child uncomfortable because he or she could not predict what you are going to do. Broken schedules, unexpected events, and changed plans disrupt the world of the only. It might be necessary for you to allow yourself to follow schedules rather than indulge your penchant for the unexpected and the unplanned in order for your only child to be comfortable.

Raising a First Born:
Trying to make your first born child feel loved could cause problems for you with him or her. Since your first born child perceives the world to be without love, he or she feels anger at your trying to make him or her feel loved. This child may feel you are trying to manipulate him or her into a denial of his or her experience of the world. If this child is of the same sex as you, the child's anger is directed outwardly at you or siblings. If the child is of the opposite sex, the anger is turned inward at self in the form of depression.

You probably try to make your first born child feel loved by softening requests so they would not offend this child, but they tend to make this child angry anyway. This reaction may not make sense to you because you talk to this child as you would like others to talk to you. For example, you would make requests kindly by saying "You need to come in now", or "Please, come in now" rather than ordering the child in. Strange as it may seem to you, your first born will respond more positively to your saying "I want you to come in now". This latter statement feels better to the first born. It does not require him or her to think the world is a loving place. Furthermore, it is assertiveness which the first born respects because you are able to say what you want. Your first born would like to be able to do that.

You could infuriate your first born by trying to placate him or her. For example, you might forbid your child to go outside but offer a substitute indoor activity. In so doing, you convey to your child you want him or her to feel loved. However, to the child it appears not only is he or she

Parenting as a Third Born

unloved, but now he or she must act as if he or she felt loved. If you think about it, you can understand why this child would get angry. It is better to simply say "No" to your first born when you must, rather than trying to make this child feel better. The child is going to be less angry than if you try to make him or her feel good.

Raising a Second Born:

You are likely to become frustrated trying to make your second born feel loved by praising him or her. Rather than feeling loved by your praise, your second born may become angry because you gloss over his or her shortcomings in giving your praise. In effect, the second born feels you are lying to him or her with such praise. Of course, you tend to get angry at your child's anger because you are not trying to deceive, only to make him or her feel good.

It is not natural for you to offer correction since you hated being put down as a child, and you avoid anything that sounds negative. But, you need to give honest feedback to your second born. Simply praising the child will not stroke him or her into feeling loved.

Raising a Third Born:

You will probably have the greatest rapport with your third born child because he or she thinks as you do. Whatever you do to make the third born feel loved probably works. And, since you do not try to tell the third born what to do, you are not apt to trigger rebelliousness in him or her.

Raising a Fourth Born:

Your fourth born child might become overly dependent on you because he or she accepts your caring. However, if you over protect this child, you probably encourage him or her to feel immature and reinforce the third born sibling's message of immaturity to the fourth born. To help this child, you need to allow him or her to face challenges rather than try and pave the way for him or her.

Parenting in Partnership

Parenting with an Only:

If you are married to an only, he or she may feel the need to enforce your will on the children because you do not. You may ask children to do something, and when they do not do what you want, you are likely to let it pass. Your only child spouse may see a need to "fix" the situation by controlling or punishing the child. You may get angry because your spouse does not let you handle it in your own nurturing way.

However, your only child spouse might provide a balance of parental control to your nurturing ways. For example, consider the difference between how you would have the children open Christmas presents and how your spouse would do it. You would probably let the children open all their gifts at the same time in a chaotic fashion. Your spouse, on the other hand, would have each child take his or her turn at opening a gift. The resulting order which maximized the enjoyment of giving and receiving gifts is probably preferable to your free-for-all style of opening the gifts. Your only child spouse could exercise the kind of control you would be loathe to use to accomplish order.

Parenting with a First Born:

If you are married to a first born, you might find the relationship strained because you are unable to make your spouse feel loved. For example, you might arrange a nice evening at home, but your spouse wants to go out; or you might prepare a good meal, but your spouse does not feel like eating. On the other hand, your spouse, being intimidated by you, may "walk carefully" to avoid provoking an attack.

Married to a first born, your children have a parent in your spouse who demands respect of them and another in yourself who nurtures. However, you as a nurturing third born, tend to obstruct your spouse's efforts at demanding respect from the children. If you are effective enough, your children may lose respect for your spouse and for authority in other settings such as school, community or church. You and your spouse need to reach an agreement between yourselves in balancing the demand for respect and nurture. You do not want your children to be caught in the disagreement.

Parenting with a Second Born:

If you are married to a second born, you tend to have the upper hand psychologically because you understand him or her on a gut level. Consequently, you probably control the parenting style in the family, but you might be frustrated by your spouse's inability to deal emotionally with the children. Realizing you want feelings, your spouse might try to create emotions which appear contrived rather than real.

Parenting with a Third Born:

Being married to another third born intensifies all the third born characteristics. Together, the two of you probably over protect your children by keeping them in an emotionally sheltered environment. You both rely on nurture to raise your children rather than exercising authority. In other words, you try to talk your children into doing what they should rather than ordering them.

This marriage provides a very comfortable atmosphere for the children but it tends to leave them vulnerable to abusive persons later in life because they expect everyone to be as nice as the two of you are. Consequently, they are sometimes unable to anticipate potential cruelty of persons they plan to marry and the mistreatment comes as a shock to them. You may need to take special pains to help them realize there is cruelty in the world.

Parenting with a Fourth Born:

If you are married to a fourth born, your spouse will probably have the upper hand over you, psychologically. This means you may not understand your spouse, you may try to make your children behave so your spouse will not get angry at them, or you may keep trying to explain your actions to him or her. If you are the wife, you may live in fear of your husband striking you. Your children may have to be more responsible than your spouse because they have to adjust to him or her. In this marriage it is important you be able to stand up to your spouse in order that neither you nor your children become victims.

Summary

In conclusion, as a third born you may be a nurturing parent who makes hard work of parenting, forgets his or her own needs while meeting the needs of family, and whose primary desire is for the children to feel loved. By understanding these traits, you may be able to allow your children to be strengthened by experiencing natural challenges while keeping them safe.

How to Love Your Children

PARENTING AS A FOURTH BORN

As a fourth born, you probably did not experience parenting by taking care of younger siblings because your older siblings were there to care for the younger children. Besides, you probably chose to pass on the feeling of being left out by ignoring your younger siblings rather than caring for them. Consequently, you did not develop a feel for parenting as a child.

Your feeling of immaturity as a fourth born can be an obstacle to parenting because without a feeling of maturity you lack the confidence necessary for parenting. Therefore, feeling immature, you defer parenting to your spouse whom you feel is better at it than you. Or, if you must parent, you probably do it from a position of immaturity, i.e., as a child would. Parenting from your own childlike position means you would tend to have unrealistic expectations of your children or to be overly permissive with them.

Since parenting can be difficult for you, you may find ways to avoid taking on the responsibilities as much as possible. You manipulate your spouse into carrying much of the load. You could use your job as a way of being gone by working extra hours. When at home, you find ways to have your spouse relate to the children instead of doing so yourself. When you leave the house, you leave the children even though you could take them with you.

On the other hand, rather than avoiding your children, your feeling of immaturity could cause you to become their playmate. To guide your children, you cajole them into behaving rather than using control techniques. For example, you might try to coax your children to go to bed rather than insisting they go to bed at an appropriate time. Consequently, your children probably stay up longer than they should. Your spouse complains he or she has another child to cope with rather than a spouse to depend on.

Raising an Only:
You may do well parenting an only child, if the child's independence relieves you of the responsibility of interacting directly, particularly as the child gets older. This child may withdraw from you, especially if you react strongly to his or her displays of emotion because of your antipathy toward anger. Your child might not use tantrums to get his or her way because he or she realizes anger is not permissible with you.

Raising a First Born:
As a fourth born, you may be hardest on your first born child. Feeling immature, you subconsciously expect this child to be more responsible than you yourself. You might require this child to parent the other children rather than doing it yourself. For example, you may expect the oldest child to comfort the younger children, to get them ready for school, or to put them to bed. Being given this role, it is understandable if your oldest child resents you or exerts more power in the family than is appropriate.

Raising a Second Born:
You would probably have the least problems with your second born child. This child's reliance on logic fits well with your propensity to analyze. Also, the second born's tendency to set aside feelings keeps this child from coming into conflict with you, especially over anger.

Raising a Third Born:
Having come to understand third borns by coping with one growing up, you probably find your third born child the easiest for you to understand, influence and control. Consequently, the third born may be your favorite, the one you reward while withholding rewards from the other children in order to teach them to be more like the third born. Naturally, this parenting behavior creates resentment in the other children toward you.

Raising a Fourth Born:

Your fourth born child is very much like yourself. Being a fourth born, you are able to detect this child's manipulative techniques better than your spouse. However, your parenting techniques may be insufficient to deal with this child, and you simply get angry at him or her.

Parenting in Partnership

Parenting with an Only:

If you are married to an only, your marriage could be difficult, not only for yourself but also for your spouse and children. As a fourth born, you are accustomed to being able to manipulate others just as you were able to manipulate your older brothers and sisters as a child. However, you never developed strategies to manipulate the only child, and the strategies you do use do not work. You cannot manage your spouse.

As a child, you learned to manipulate others by presenting yourself as a victim or potential victim. For example, you might have said "Nobody wants me" at which everyone would protest "We want you" and would do what you wanted. As an adult, you might use this technique on your spouse by saying "If you don't want me to stay just tell me to leave and I will leave". Other birth orders feel compelled to say "You don't have to go" but an only is apt to say "If you want to leave, then leave". To your frustration, your strategies do not produce the anticipated results with an only. Consequently, you may be angry at your only child spouse much of the time.

On the other hand, your only child spouse desires to know what you want, what you have decided, and what you expect. These are questions which you find difficult to answer because you keep analyzing even after you make a decision. Your spouse does not recognize your need to analyze nor can he or she tolerate your indecisiveness, becoming as frustrated with you as you are with him or her.

This is, of course, a difficult family relationship for the children. They usually find themselves sympathizing with one parent and angry at the other.

Parenting with a First Born:

If your spouse is first born, he or she tends to have the upper hand in the relationship. This makes yours a fairly compatible marriage. Your spouse can tolerate, perhaps even enjoy, your analyzing so you feel satisfied he or she listens to you. Also, your spouse tends to accept your manipulation so you experience less frustration.

Parenting with a Second Born:
If your spouse is second born, you usually have the upper hand, psychologically. Your analyzing creates logic which seems reasonable to your spouse, enabling you to influence your second born spouse to your ways of thinking in most areas. Consequently, parenting is probably done your way in your family. In fact, in a dispute between you and the children, your spouse probably takes your side.

Parenting with a Third Born:
If your spouse is third born, you definitely have the upper hand because you are psychologically able to manipulate your spouse. When your spouse was growing up, he or she could overpower the fourth born and therefore did not have to understand him or her. Consequently, if your spouse is going to dominate you as an adult third born, he or she has to use force rather than manipulation. He or she probably does this by attacking.

Being married to a third born, you may experience conflict because of differences in communication techniques. You speak tentatively because you expect to continue analyzing but your spouse speaks in conclusions. Each of you interprets the other according to your own way of talking. You perceive what your spouse says to be only a prelude and, because he or she has nothing more to say, you imagine him or her to be superficial. Since your spouse expects you to speak in conclusions, he or she takes the first thing you say at face value without listening to what else you have to say. Communication between the two of you may be constant misinterpretation.

Strangely enough, the children seem to do well even with the conflict. Perhaps they are supported emotionally by the third born making them feel loved and your desire to be a companion. If the children have to choose between one parent or another in a divorce, they may choose either one. In some families, they feel closer to the fourth born and in others they feel closer to the third born.

Parenting with a Fourth Born:
Two fourth borns married to each other tend to get along well but when they have difficulties they stop talking to each other. It is typical in these marriages for them to go without communicating for days. Because both parents struggle with immaturity, it is also typical for the children to assume a lot of responsibility by default.

Summary

As a fourth born, your parenting depends on how well you have come to terms with the feeling of immaturity. If you feel grown up, accept yourself as an adult, and relate to others on an equal basis, you parent better than if you have to struggle with feeling like a child among adults.

How to Love Your Children

WHEN NOTHING WORKS

You have tried everything and nothing has made a difference with your child. He or she continues to misbehave, to be destructive, to use alcohol or drugs, or to be truant. You are at your wits' end. What do you do?

When you realize nothing works, get professional help. There comes a time when parenting may no longer be a do-it-yourself project.

The strategies in this book are for families which are healthy enough to use them. They can be used if there is already a basis for improvement rather than a sense of desperation. If you are desperate, get help.

If your family is basically healthy but nothing seems to work, take a closer look at what you yourself are doing. You may be unconsciously introducing elements into your communication which subvert the effectiveness of what you are trying to do. If you use this book only to manipulate others, you may not be able to accomplish what you want. Examine yourself if things are not working the way you want them to work.

Use this book to understand yourself, your spouse and your family. By so doing, you enable yourself to use birth order interventions and affirmations naturally, easily and successfully.

If you have problems which prevent you from applying what you have learned in this book, you may want to refer to the book, THE BIRTH ORDER CHALLENGE, by the author. It contains therapy for each of the birth orders in the form of double bind questions which cause changes to happen on the subconscious level. The book is available from the publisher and ordering information is provided at the end of this book.

How to Love Your Children

APPENDIX

ONLY CHILD CHARACTERISTICS

Childhood Problems:
  How to play alone without feeling lonely.
  How to cope with intrusion.
Life Decision:
  Anyone can interfere with me anytime.
Felt Loss: Freedom.
Coping Mechanisms:
  Creates imaginary friends .
  Develops two speeds.
Concept of Justice: Equal treatment.
Thinking Pattern: Organizing.
Communication: Tells stories.
Problem Solving Technique: Organizing.
Internal Behaviors:
  Thinks with feelings.
    Makes decisions on anticipated feelings.
    Checks emotions first before deciding.
  Fears being intruded upon by others.
    Dislikes surprises which intrude.
    Braces against intrusion.
  Does not understand others.
    Sees others as imaginary.
    Projects self into another's place to understand.
  Intrudes on self by
    Thinking about work while playing.
    Thinking about play while working.
  Feels life is all work and no play.
    Divides tasks into
      Things that have to be done.
      Things that one feels like doing.
  Feels burdened by things that have to be done.
Worries.

Wants to do things correctly.
Borrows feelings from others.
    Feels bad when others feel bad.
    Feels good when others feel good.
Fears disappointment.
    May adopt pessimism to minimize disappointment.
    May refuse to make plans to escape disappointment.
External Behaviors:
    Organizes.
    Expresses self emotionally.
        Is animated in conversation.
        Puts feeling into stories.
    Reacts rather than interacts.
        Responds to feeling with logic.
        Responds to logic with feeling.
    Interrupts others.
        Projects motives, feelings and thoughts on others.
        Makes assumptions rather than listening.
    Does not listen to problems well.
        Wants to fix the problem, or
        Wants to correct the person's feelings.
    Procrastinates.
        Waits for enough time to do a task all at once.
        Does lesser tasks first.
        Finishes task under pressure of time.
    Refuses requests at first but may reconsider later.
    Likes to spend time alone at home.
Means of loving: Worry.
Therapeutic questions* to enhance loving: Is it okay for you to listen to yourself rather than worrying? Is okay for you to listen to others instead of worrying?

FIRST BORN CHARACTERISTICS

Childhood Problem: Loss of love to the baby.
Life Decision: "No one loves me".
Felt Loss: Love.
Coping Mechanism: Seeks conditional love.
Concept of Justice: People should get what they deserve.
Thinking Pattern: Rehearsal.
Communication: Tries to impress.
Problem Solving Technique: Cover-up.
Internal Behaviors:
    Believes others do not care about him or her.
    Does not care about self.

Appendix

    Finds it difficult to express love to others.
    Creates good feelings for self by daydreaming of future.
    Is often dissatisfied with present.
    Feels relief rather than joy over accomplishments.
    Is unaware of own wants, thoughts or feelings.
        Experiences compulsive wanting of things.
        Does not enjoy things once obtained.
    Does not understand others.
        Is unable to anticipate what they will do.
        Is unable to manipulate others.
    Experiences Damocles Sword effect.
        Believes there is no mercy for him or her.
        Experiences feelings of guilt.
External Behaviors:
    Commonly says "I don't know".
    Hints at what he or she wants.
    Seeks respect at home.
        Demands agreement from family members.
        Demands immediate obedience.
    Tries to impress peers.
    Tries to get approval from authority figures.
    Compromises readily away from home.
    Fears offending others.
Means of loving: Agreeing.
Therapeutic question* to enhance loving: Is it okay for you to be honest with people rather than agreeing with them?

SECOND BORN CHARACTERISTICS

Childhood Problems:
    Made to look inadequate by the first born.
    Feelings ignored by first born.
Life Decision: "I cannot do anything well enough".
Felt Loss: Emotion.
Coping Mechanisms:
    Seeking perfection in limited areas of endeavor.
    Avoiding emotion through being rational.
Concept of Justice: The end justifies the means.
Thinking Pattern: Evaluation.
Communication: Expresses judgments.
Characteristic Phrases:
    "I would appreciate it if you would...".
    "That's not necessary".
Problem Solving Technique:
Determine who is responsible.

How to Love Your Children

Internal Behaviors:
  Feels inadequate.
  Likes projects, dislikes goals.
  Notices flaws.
  Is sensitive to criticism.
  Dislikes making others angry.
  Seeks to create peace.
  Acts as a mediator.
  Ignores own feelings.
External Behaviors:
  Focuses on details to achieve perfection.
  Ignores feelings.
    Expects feelings to be understood through actions.
    Responds to feelings with logic.
  Offers correction.
  Often communicates by writing rather than talking.
  Tends to become critical when stressed.
  Will pass on criticisms to one being criticized.
    Will "tell" on others.
    Criticizes indirectly rather than directly.
  Praises a person indirectly by telling someone else.
  May be overwhelmed with emotions when under stress.
  Loyal to family.
  Dislikes deadlines.
    May finish assignments in advance of deadlines or,
    May do assignments at last minute.
Means of loving: By giving constructive criticism.
Therapeutic questions* to enhance loving: Is it okay for you to think about how you feel instead of giving correction? Is it okay for you to think about how others feel instead of giving correction?

THIRD BORN CHARACTERISTICS

Childhood Problems: Being put down by second born.
Life Decision: "People can get to me anytime they want".
Felt Loss: Justice.
Coping Mechanism: Not to let anything bother him or her.
Concept of Justice: Robin Hood justice, help the victims.
Thinking Pattern: Comparing.
Communication: Talks in conclusions.
Characteristic Phrase: "No Problem".
Problem Solving Technique: Attack.
Internal Behaviors:
  Feels vulnerable.

Appendix

Fears fear.
Treats fear as an enemy.
Lacks a defense system.
Cannot stand up for him or herself.
Wants to be emotionally strong.
May experience panic or anxiety attacks.
Dislikes being ordered to do something.
    Likes being asked.
    Likes to hear "please".
Fears boredom.
Sensitive to having ideas rejected.
External Behaviors:
    If fearless,
        Acts emotionally strong.
        Does scary things fearlessly.
        Accepts dares.
        May be rebellious.
    If fearful,
        Acts fearful.
        Refuses to do scary things.
        Withdraws into a safe environment.
    May not defend him or herself.
    May seek strength in religion.
    May seek strength in motivation.
    May get bored easily.
        Does not like predictability.
        Does not like repetitiveness.
    May act as a rescuer.
        May befriend lower class persons.
        May rescue animals.
        May collect broken things.
    Creates ideas.
    Uses humor to establish distance.
    Likes to give advice.
        May enjoy solving problems for others.
        Resents having ideas rejected.
    Never wants to be early.
    Goes off on a tangent easily.
    Leaves out details when talking.
    May explode in anger if pushed far enough.
Means of Loving: Pleasing others.
Therapeutic Questions* to enhance loving: Is it okay for you to be fair to yourself rather than trying to please other people? Is it okay for you to be fair to others rather than trying to please them?

FOURTH BORN CHARACTERISTICS

Childhood Problems: Feeling unwanted, immature.
Life Decisions:
  "I'm never going to be grown up enough".
  No one wants me.
Felt Loss: Trust.
Coping Mechanisms:
  To deal with immaturity
    May give in to it.
    May choose to overcome it by
      doing difficult things.
      or by not listening to self.
  To deal with rejection
    May choose to stay outside a group or,
    May become an entertainer to be accepted.
Concept of Justice: Retaliation.
Thinking Pattern: Analysis
Communication: Speaks in Introductions.
Characteristic Phrase: "I don't care".
Problem Solving Technique: Deny the problem.
Internal Behaviors:
  Does not listen to self.
    Experiences confusion under stress.
    Does not rely on own judgment.
  Believes no one listens to him or her.
  Does not listen to others.
  Feels excluded by others.
    Feels jealousy when a friend has a friend.
    Needs a special invitation to join a group.
  Very sensitive to blame.
    Berates self for being stupid.
    Seeks for a way to blame someone else.
  Resents being used.
    Fears being used when asked for something.
    Is paranoid about others taking advantage.
  Is unable to reach conclusions.
    Keeps analyzing.
    Changes his or her mind frequently.
  Values logic over feelings.
    Sees feelings as undependable.
    Waits for feelings to change in others.
External Behaviors:
  May exclude self from groups.

Appendix

May talk loudly, use profanity, threaten or strike.
May not remember having said something.
Tries to confuse others when confronted.
Manipulates others by presenting self as a victim.
May interfere with a friend's other relationships.
Has unrealistic expectations of others.
Sees problems as either insignificant
 or insurmountable.
May have difficulty having fun.
May sabotage a task when asked to do something.
Clams up when challenged, shrugs shoulders.
May be a bully in family relationships.
Hates laziness.
May relate well to children.
Means of Loving: Giving gifts.
Therapeutic questions* to enhance loving: Is it okay for you to trust yourself rather than giving things to other people? Is it okay for you to trust other people rather than giving them things?

*For information on the Therapeutic Question refer to The Birth Order Challenge by Clifford E. Isaacson (1991: The Upper Des Moines Counseling Center, Box 235, Algona, Iowa 50511)

How to Love Your Children

ABOUT THE AUTHOR

Clifford E. Isaacson is a United Methodist Minister who served churches for twenty-five years before leaving the pastorate to do full time counseling. In 1986, he helped found the Upper Des Moines Counseling Center, Inc. of Algona, Iowa which he serves as a counselor and its executive director.

While taking training in Transactional Analysis, he learned the concept of life scripts. This concept suggests that people live as if they were taking part in a play rather than choosing their behavior freely. By comparing life scripts to birth order positions, he discovered that birth order consists of five well defined personality types. Over the past twenty-two years during which he conducted over 19,000 counseling sessions, he refined the birth order concept to what it is today.

During his years of counseling, he discovered that certain ways of phrasing statements, doing things and confronting persons according to birth order communicated better than others. He discovered that each birth order personality requires a different approach in order to produce a hearing, to create rapport, and to encourage responsible behavior.

Countless people have used his discoveries to improve communications between couples, within families, and in the business place. His methods have proved especially useful in direct selling, teaching and medicine.

How to Love Your Children is the third book about birth order by Mr. Isaacson. The others are a self-help book entitled **The Birth Order Challenge** and an introductory book entitled **Understanding Yourself Through Birth Order.**

He is married, and with his wife Kathleen has five children and nine grandchildren. They continue to make their home in Algona where he served the First United Methodist Church as its pastor for seven years before establishing the counseling center.

How to Love Your Children

- I N D E X -

Abuse, 48, 60, 75, 78
Admiration, 30, 31, 32, 34, 35, 37, 38, 42
Adopted, 8
Advice, 13, 27, 125
Age Difference, 9, 11
Aggressive, 42, 67
Alone, 7, 8, 12, 15, 16, 19, 24, 25, 53, 75, 89, 107, 121, 122
Analyze, 76, 103, 114, 115
Anger, 2, 15, 18, 41, 52, 57, 61, 62, 65, 82, 86, 89, 92, 102, 106, 108, 109, 114, 125
Appearance, 46
Appreciate, 6, 39, 40, 54, 98, 103, 123
Approval, 30, 31, 32, 34, 35, 102, 103, 123
Argue, 25, 39, 47, 87, 98, 105
Assertive, 42, 57, 68
Attacks, 60, 61, 62, 125
Authority, 31, 87, 98, 105, 110, 111, 123
Blame, 33, 78, 85, 126
Blended Families, 8
Boredom, 61, 69, 125
Boundaries, 27
Buffer, 62
Bully, 69, 78, 126
Cautious, 26, 71, 106
Challenge, 39, 60, 71, 83, 84, 95, 99
Chores, 12, 15, 19
Command, 67, 88
Compare, 62
Compatible, 99, 116
Compete, 5, 9
Compliments, 47, 102
Compromise, 33
Conclusions, 46, 63, 103, 116, 124, 126
Conditional, 30, 32, 34, 35, 38, 39, 122
Confront, 2, 6, 24, 38, 54, 55, 68
Confusion 74, 84, 126
Consequences, 48, 97, 101
Correction, 13, 26, 49, 52, 53, 102, 109, 124

Criticism, 19, 41, 49, 52, 54, 57, 92, 102, 124
Creative, 62, 64, 67
Damocles Sword, 32, 123
Dare, 60
Daydreams, 32
Deserve, 24, 33, 122
Disappointment, 18, 27, 107, 122
Discipline, 1, 62, 90, 93, 106
Dramatic, 16, 17
Deadlines, 19, 48, 124
Defense, 49, 59, 61, 62, 66, 68, 78, 86, 104, 125
Depression, 108
Disagree, 35, 38, 40, 92, 104
Disobey, 39
Distract, 62
Dysfunctional, 7
Embarrassment, 63
Empathy, 63, 65
Escape, 5, 6, 15, 18, 26, 27, 41, 55, 71, 74, 88, 101, 102, 107, 122
Evaluate, 18, 42, 48, 49
Excitement, 61, 69
Fantasy, 34
Fearful, 60, 61, 62, 70, 76, 90, 97, 98, 125
Fearless, 60, 61, 64, 71, 90, 97, 98, 105, 125
Fight, 68, 69, 108
Force, 10, 23, 26, 59, 71, 74, 85, 86, 92, 103, 104, 105, 116
Friends, 12, 15, 16, 17, 34, 37, 38, 40, 47, 63, 64, 69, 76, 90, 96, 121
Goals, 47, 48, 89, 90, 98, 124
Guilty, 41
Happy, 16, 27, 38, 41, 42, 102
Harassment, 69
Hit, 78
Humor, 49, 62, 63, 64, 71, 125
Ideas, 17, 18, 27, 49, 59, 62, 63, 64, 66, 67, 70, 71, 75, 76, 90, 125
Ignorance, 21, 31, 76, 77, 97
Imaginary, 8, 15, 16, 17, 19, 24, 27, 121
Immature, 7, 9, 73, 75, 76, 83, 84, 109, 113, 114, 126
Impress, 30, 31, 40, 122, 123
Inadequate, 9, 29, 45, 49, 59, 98, 102, 123, 124

Include, 14, 35, 82, 83, 85
Inferiority, 69
Interrupt, 17, 76
Intimidation, 60, 61, 71
Intrusive, 8, 13, 14, 22, 23, 26, 27, 88, 92, 98, 108
Inventors, 63
Invulnerable, 60
Justice, 13, 65, 78, 87, 88, 92, 121, 122, 123, 124, 126
Lonely, 7, 8, 12, 15, 24, 121
Loyalty, 56, 71
Lying, 32, 104, 109
Manipulate, 97, 103, 108, 113, 115, 116, 119, 123
Mercy, 35, 38, 123
Mistake, 26, 82
Nasty, 49
Necessity, 28, 41, 55, 105
Notes, 48
Obedience, 62, 91, 95, 96, 97, 123
Offend, 42, 66, 108
Organize, 8, 13, 28, 90, 92
Panic, 62, 125
Peer, 35, 90
Perfection, 46, 48, 49, 52, 53, 56, 57, 103, 123, 124
Pitfalls, 49
Please, 3, 23, 30, 31, 67, 71, 108, 125
Pout, 31, 39
Praise, 32, 34, 38, 49, 53, 102, 109
Prioritize, 33
Privacy, 21, 22 32, 34
Procrastinate, 19, 48, 77
Promises, 1, 14, 23
Punishment, 5, 15, 39
Rational, 22, 24, 50, 55, 90, 92, 104, 123
Rebellious, 64, 125
Rehearsing, 34
Rejected, 24, 29, 42, 62, 66, 67, 70, 77, 125
Rescue, 63, 64, 125
Respect, 30, 31, 33, 34, 35, 38, 40, 91, 92, 95, 96, 97, 98, 99, 105, 110, 123
Responsible, 24, 93, 111, 114, 123, 129
Ridicule, 9, 34, 61
Schedule, 13, 14, 23, 90, 96

Secretive, 77
Security, 61, 66, 67, 70, 71
Seduce, 33
Self-disciplined, 25, 47, 106
Self-esteem, 43, 48, 53, 82
Self-help, 6, 129
Strong, 16, 60, 65, 69, 73, 96, 99, 114, 125
Stupid, 34, 126
Surprise, 14, 21, 23, 24, 37, 38, 40, 43, 53, 54
Sympathy, 47, 66, 71
Tantrums, 14, 18, 114
Teasing, 59
Twins, 8
Unfair, 33, 38, 49, 98, 106
Unwanted, 8, 9, 12, 73, 75, 79, 81, 102, 126
Victims, 63, 64, 111, 124
Victimized, 2, 68, 84
Vulnerability, 9, 64, 65, 71, 73
Weak, 60, 70
Withdrawal, 24, 68, 86
Worry, 18, 19, 26, 42, 62, 90, 122

ORDERING INFORMATION

The following books by Clifford E. Isaacson may be ordered from the Upper Des Moines Counseling Center:

HOW TO LOVE YOUR CHILDREN: Birth Order For Parents (1992), 128 pages.
$7.95 (Paper) ISBN 0-945156-03-0
This book describes birth order and how it can be used to communicate with children to get them to listen, to make them feel loved, and to encourage them to behave responsibly.

THE BIRTH ORDER CHALLENGE: Expanding Your Horizons (1991), 183 pages.
$19.95 (Hardbound) ISBN 0-945156-01-4
$11.95 (Paper) ISBN 0-945156-02-2
This book describes birth order, defines problems related to birth order, and helps the reader experience counseling through counselor-client dialogues.

UNDERSTANDING YOURSELF THROUGH BIRTH ORDER (1988), 120 pages.
$7.95 (Paper) ISBN 0-945156-00-6
This book introduces the concept of birth order, explains how birth order happens, accounts for exceptions to birth order, and defines how birth order affects family relationships, marital harmony and emotional health.

These books may be ordered from:

UPPER DES MOINES COUNSELING CENTER, INC.
Box 235
Algona, Iowa 50511

Please add postage of $1.05 for the first book, $.50 for each additional book. Iowa residents please add sales tax.

389-1
5-42
CC